Personal Computer: A New Tool for Ministers

PERSONAL COMPUTER A NEW TOOL FOR MINISTERS

RUSSELL H. DILDAY, JR.

BROADMAN PRESS
Nashville, Tennessee

4231-11
ISBN: 0-8054-3111-X

Dewey Decimal Classification Number: 253.028
Subject Headings: MINISTERS // COMPUTERS
Library of Congress Catalog Number: 84-20360

Printed in the United States of America

Library of Congress Cataloging in Publication Data

Dilday, Russell H.
Personal computer.

1. Pastoral theology—Data processing. 2. Church management—Data processing. I. Title.
BV652.77.D55 1985 253'.028'54 84-20360
ISBN 0-8054-3111-X (pbk.)

To Betty

who in our marriage has personified the ideal of
"user friendly compatibility"
and whose
"megabite capacity" for encouragement
has helped keep me at the task

Contents

Introduction

Technology is not a familiar world to me. Microchips, ROMs, RAMs, and bytes have always been "faraway places with strange-sounding names," and when in the company of someone who speaks "computerese" I have usually tried to redirect the conversation into the more comfortable jargon of theology.

But here I am at the keyboard of a TRS-80 Model 4P computer punching away at the buttons and watching the silver letters jog across the screen forming the words of this paragraph as they go. It's incredible! When I type to the edge of the display screen (or "page" as I used to call it), I have no need to return the carriage or push the return bar like on a typewriter. The sentence automatically "wraps around" and continues on the next line.

Forget correction tape, white fluid, or rubber erasers. All I have to do is back up the cursor on the screen to the error and type it correctly. Or, using the word processing program, I can delete, exchange, insert, or otherwise manipulate the letters until they're just right. Now, no matter what I may be composing, I no longer use the yellow legal pads and pencils to which I have become addicted over the years. Instead, I flip on the Model 4P, load the SuperSCRIPSIT word processing program, and peck away freely on the keyboard without worrying about errors. The computer has spoiled me with its automatic features.

Admittedly, I am still a newcomer to this unfamiliar world

of writing on a video monitor. But that's just the point. If I can learn to do it, you can learn to do it, too. The main purpose of this book is to encourage the "nonuser" to jump in, join the computer generation, and discover how a pastor or a church staff member can employ the personal computer in the work of the ministry. If you're already one of the initiated who owns or has access to computer hardware, then I hope you'll find some new ideas or applications in the book that will enhance your work in the church.

Before moving to chapter 1, let's discuss something that is as widespread as the common cold: *Computer Phobia.* For a number of reasons, almost everyone has a little fear of computers at the beginning.

You may have been billed incorrectly by a company, and when you telephoned to correct the mistake you were told it was "a computer error." The bill kept coming, and you kept calling, and pretty soon "the computer" was threatening to sue you. That's reason enough to shy away from any contact with the monsters!

Or maybe your fear stems from the foreboding anxiety brought on by the report that someone might push the wrong button on a computer in Siberia or Colorado and blow up the world.

In his book *1984* George Orwell predicted that "Big Brother" would use giant computers to watch everyone in a government-controlled society. The prospects of this kind of computer abuse is a specter with real possibilities today, but the problem is not computers. It's the people who operate them. While the government may be collecting more information about people than is necessary to run the government, and while it is possible for computer security to be broken and the information abused, the machines themselves are not the cause of this abuse. We must learn to control those who are responsible and not let our fears lead us to reject computer technology.

More likely, computer phobia is the common fear that we'll

feel stupid as we confront such an intelligent machine. But remember, the machine is not intelligent. The computer can do nothing without you as the brain that operates it.

If there is anything to fear, it's computer illiteracy, especially on the part of ministers who ought to be not only the most-dedicated followers of Christ, but the best-trained as well. The pastor or staff member who doesn't become "literate" in at least the basics of microcomputer use will be left behind in our rapidly developing world.

If I were beginning again in the pastorate to which God called me thirty years ago, I would eagerly apply computer technology in my work. I would thank God for providentially providing such an efficient instrument. Could this application of the microcomputer in ministry be an example of what Paul had in mind when he commanded us to "redeem the time" or "make the most of the time in which you live" (see Col. 4:5)?

My thanks to several who helped complete the book: Nancy Morgan, Stormy Ratliff, and Sharon Beougher for assistance in manuscript preparation; Terry Bratton for technical advice; and the personnel of Broadman Press for those mysterious "behind the scenes" services that bring these pages finally to print.

I want to emphasize to my readers that this book was written within the framework of my own experience and study. For example, throughout this book I have referred to the Radio Shack TRS-80 Model 4P, software and other items for this computer, and various products from other manufacturers. In doing so, I have written from the viewpoint of my own equipment or materials with which I am familiar. Although I refer to specific brand names, I want my readers to understand that I am not recommending that they purchase any item mentioned in this book. Many items are available from numerous manufacturers, and I have described some of them to show that computers are effective tools. When you are ready to make a purchase, buy what suits your needs. The principles identified in this volume can be applied to your equipment.

Furthermore, you would expect me to be partial to Southwestern Baptist Theological Seminary, and I am sure my bias is transparent. Again, I am writing about areas with which I am most familiar. Some of our other Southern Baptist schools already make extensive use of computer technology, and others will join them in the future.

1
Getting Started

I pulled out the mixture control on the instrument panel to the "full lean" position, and the engine of the Cessna 172 sputtered to a stop. The FAA flight examiner unlatched the door and, without saying a word, stepped out of the plane and walked around the parking ramp to the left door where I was still seated behind the wheel. Looking through the papers on his clipboard for what seemed like an hour, he finally scribbled his signature on the temporary form. Then with a smile he extended his right hand in congratulations. I was officially licensed to fly a single-engine aircraft!

It all began two years earlier on a private plane trip from Houston to Dallas. The pilot in whose plane I was riding seemed older to me. Now that I think about it, he was probably the same age I am now. Nevertheless, about an hour into the flight I had a frightening thought. What if this "older" friend were to suffer an attack of some kind? What if he were to faint or otherwise become incapacitated? What would I do? The answer was clear. I would be helpless because I knew absolutely nothing about flying.

As usual, we arrived safely, but I resolved to learn at least some basics of flying. Who could tell? I might have to handle some unforeseen emergency when flying with someone "older" in the future.

There was a general aviation airport not far from our house, and there my flying education started. Purchasing every flight instruction manual the airport had for sale, I began to read about a subject that was as foreign to me as a new language. Aeronautics, instruments, meteorology, navigation, radio use, and regulations were all unfamiliar subjects, but fascinating. I found it difficult to put the books down.

As in all good teaching manuals, there were test questions at the end of each chapter. Incorrect answers sent me back to read again the text and illustrations. When I encountered concepts I couldn't understand (and that happened frequently), a member of our church, an airline pilot, would supply simple explanations.

So with the help of my dog-eared flying manuals and my pilot friend who was as patient as my manuals were dog-eared, I began to develop a fairly good working knowledge of this new subject. In fact, bolstered by newfound confidence, I stopped by the FAA office one day, took the written examination for the private pilot's license, and made a surprising grade of 96. And that was without a single flying lesson, without ever having had my hands on the controls of a plane!

Over the next twenty-four months my friend the airline pilot, who was also a certified instructor, gave me flying lessons in a Cessna 172. No pilot can ever forget that memorable day when the instructor says, "I believe you're ready." I let him out on the parking ramp, taxied out to the end of the runway, and took off. Alone! Never is the word *solo* used more vividly than when it describes one's first experience alone at the controls of an airplane!

The next time my instructor said, "I believe you're ready" was months later. It was time to take the certification ride with an FAA flight inspector. If I passed, he would "sign me off" as a licensed pilot. I did, and he did, and the paper was folded carefully into my billfold to prove it. The proverb was wrong. One *can* teach an old dog new tricks. In the words of an old, old joke: "A few months ago I couldn't even spell 'pilot' and now I are one."

Having accomplished such an unlikely goal, it's no surprise that when computers became my new fascination, I remembered how I "taught myself" to fly. Why couldn't the same method of self-learning be employed with computers? I decided to try.

While it's not a matter of life and death, like finding yourself uninformed in an airplane with an "older" pilot, learning about computers has suddenly become an urgent priority for practically everyone.

The computer is beginning to do for the human mind what the engine did years ago for the muscles. It has been described as the most powerful tool created to serve the individual who seeks to understand the world. That students in their basic education become acquainted with the computer is now a no more radical thought than the proposition that they be able to read and write. Consequently, most public schools are adding "computer literacy" to their curricula.

In *Megatrends,* John Naisbitt announced the arrival of "the information age" with his surprising statement:

> Now more than 65 percent of us work with information as programmers, teachers, clerks, secretaries, accountants, stockbrokers, managers, insurance people, bureaucrats, lawyers, bankers, and technicians. And many more workers hold information jobs within manufacturing companies. Most Americans spend their time creating, processing, or distributing information.[1]

The computer explosion is both the evidence and one of the causes of this revolutionary change. Predictably, many social analysts agree that the computer is the single greatest factor impacting these last years of the twentieth century.

Surely modern ministers, desiring to excel in what God called them to do, will learn as much as possible about this new technology and harness the best of it for the ministry. But can an individual (usually an "older" individual) with absolutely no training or experience in computers become an effective user? My own experience of self-learning leads me to answer yes.

With my curiosity in full gear, I began to read. Have you explored the computer section of your neighborhood bookstore lately? If not, you're in for a surprise. You'll discover it is one of the largest sections in the establishment and is probably near the front to be as accessible as possible. I found several helpful books with titles such as *Computers for Everybody, The Personal Computer Handbook, The Illustrated Computer Dictionary, Your First Computer, A Simplified Guide to Micro-Computers, The Plain Brown Wrapper Book of Computers,* and *1001 Things to Do With Your Personal Computer.* Repeating my pattern in learning to fly, I began to devour new information that was as foreign to me as the aeronautical terms in the flight manuals.

The library also had some helpful books. However, the ones I checked out were slightly behind the times; the bookstore selections were more up-to-date. This is a rapidly-changing field.

Since I travel frequently, the airport magazine stand became another helpful source of information. Maybe I hadn't noticed it before, but now it seemed computer periodicals dominated the selections. *Popular Computing, Personal Computing, Infoworld, Byte, Creative Computing, Micro-Computing, Family Computing, Interface Age, Desktop Computing, Home Computer Magazine* are examples of a multitude on the market today. In addition, I found helpful information in business publications and newsmagazines and in some local newspapers which run feature articles for beginners. Of course, all of these sources recommended still others which could be ordered.

The next step in my "do-it-yourself" course in computer literacy was to visit the friendly neighborhood computer shop. You'll find some of them selling only one brand such as Apple, IBM, or Radio Shack. But others offer a variety which can be compared side by side. While they may be somewhat biased since they want to sell you a machine, most of the salespersons I talked to were patient and helpful. Understanding the predicament of an uninformed beginner, they resisted the temptation to dazzle me with their technical language or to laugh at my dumb questions (at least not until I'd left the store).

One of the beginner books I bought told how to turn on a computer and try out a few simple routines so that when you went into a store the salesperson would know you were not a total ignoramus. But I decided it would be more embarrassing when the clerk discovered I was completely over my head after the first few taps on the keyboard. I decided to be myself, a "know-nothing" who was genuinely interested in learning from scratch. This approach worked well and after each visit, my knowledge grew.

The first thing I thought I needed to learn was, "What kind of equipment should I secure?" Two things quickly became clear. The market is flooded with various brands, sizes, and types of computers and the scene is changing almost daily. Whoever called it a "computer explosion" must have been the same person who named the beginner pilot's first flight a "solo." It is a vivid and accurate description. The computer population is indeed exploding. Just when I thought I knew which models a company was selling, another more-advanced and less-expensive machine would be announced. Or worse, without any concern for my growing frustration, the company would go out of business.

I felt an irresistible temptation to wait another month for the prices to go down or a better model to be released. That's when I received some timely advice: "Go ahead and jump in with the best decision at the time. If you wait, you'll stand around forever watching the 'merry-go-round' and never climbing on board for the ride."

A newspaper article entitled "Buying a Personal Computer" was helpful because it compared by chart and easy-to-understand language what the author considered the top seven brands. I narrowed the choices to three or four types and then picked one and plunged in. What factors should be considered in a purchase?

First, you must decide what primary uses you're likely to make of the new equipment. That's a little difficult to do when you know very little about what *can* be done on a computer. Let me shorten your procedure a little by suggesting that as a minister using the computer as a personal resource in your ministry, your most likely applications will be:

Word Processing (Writing sermons, letters, articles, books, etc.)

Filing (record keeping, sorting, recalling facts, etc.)

Financial Planning (Spreadsheets, what-if calculations, budgets, etc.)

Accessing Data Bases (For research information, electronic mail)

Family Purposes (Education, entertainment, etc.)

Most personal computers can handle all these functions through the use of innumerable software packages available at most computer stores. But that's jumping too far ahead. How to choose equipment will be discussed in another chapter. The point I want to make now is that as you read various articles and books, you will soon gain sufficient orientation for a decision about equipment. But on with the "do-it-yourself" story of computer education.

Believe it or not, the equipment I bought was easy to assemble. When I unpacked my Radio Shack TRS-80 Model 4P, I readily recognized the various pieces from the reading I had done. The computer itself was a unit with a screen, a keyboard, familiar-looking switches, and two unfamiliar slots beside the screen that looked like the openings in an electric toaster. There was also a little box called a modem which I knew from my reading somehow connected the computer to the telephone, and a printer that looked like an electric typewriter without a keyboard.

Even without referring to the instruction booklets, it was obvious which part should be connected to which other part. In a matter of minutes, I had the computer hooked up to the printer and the modem. Next, I plugged the power cords into the electric socket behind my desk (anyone who can plug in an electric toaster can plug in a computer).

Then came that moment not unlike the first time I turned on the ignition switch in the Cessna 172. I turned on the switch on the computer! The printer buzzed a few seconds. The little red lights on the toaster slots flickered momentarily, and a message flashed on the screen, "The Floppy Disk Drive Is Not Ready." It was very clear that the disk drive was not the only thing that was not ready. I couldn't make my new computer do anything else. No matter what buttons on the keyboard I pushed, nothing happened. Obviously I needed to do some more reading. I turned it off and went back to the task of self-learning.

Fortunately, I have a friend who is a computer expert. Risking a strain on his patience and our friendship, I have hounded him with questions. This was especially helpful after I began using my TRS-80 Model 4P. If you have no such access to personal advice, there are informal "users groups" in most cities organized around the major brands of computers. (For example, a local newspaper column announced a "Mid-Cities TRS-80 Users Group" which meets second and fourth Tuesdays at 7:00 PM.) Dealers can tell you how to contact the proper organization in your community, and you'll discover these people are eager to help.

I've found that users are often well ahead of the sales force at the computer store and sometimes ahead of the experts at the manufacturing plants when it comes to answering practical questions about using the machines. Low-cost or free software written by members of users groups is also made available at their meetings. Isn't it interesting how a spirit of comradeship or esprit de corps develops among a group of people who share a common interest?

Although I've never taken advantage of them, most companies offer free instruction courses with a computer purchase. They also encourage phone calls when you have questions about the use of your computer. I have used this last service frequently.

Another suggestion: classes in computers are offered by most area colleges. These are frequently scheduled at night or on Saturdays and are relatively inexpensive, especially if offered by a public institution. A junior college in Fort Worth, Texas, for example, advertised in the local newspaper forty courses in computer science offered to the public. Course titles included:

Computers Are Ridiculously Simple
Introduction to Computers
Word Processing on the Microcomputer
Selecting Your Personal Computer

Another advertisement described a seminar called "Introduction to Computers—A hands-on, nontechnical workshop for everybody who knows zero about computers." There are probably similar educational opportunities in your area.

Don't overlook organizations such as the American Management Association which provide seminars designed for people with various levels of experience. I took a three-day seminar on the use of computerized spreadsheets for budget planning offered by the AMA and found it very helpful. However, this was after I had begun using my personal computer and knew at least some of the questions I needed to have answered.

Whether you're shopping for a computer or trying to learn more about the model you already have, computer shows can be an eye-opening experience. These exhibits are usually annual and last only a few days, but they provide an excellent opportunity to examine a variety of products under a single roof. Furthermore, you get the chance to try out various computers and software and to see the latest offerings on the market. Sometimes you can find good bargains at shows, especially on the last day, when many exhibitors would rather sell a product than take it home.

Finally, when you purchase a computer, a printer, other peripheral equipment, or a software package, you'll receive operation manuals that will be helpful. These manuals are known in computer circles as "documentation." While considerable improvements have been made in the last few years, I have found most manuals to be poorly written, usually in technical language a beginner can't understand, and often with mistakes which must be corrected before the manual can be used.

The first manual I examined came with a TRS-80 Model 3 and was practically unusable. Here's an example of the foggy style so typical of computer documentation:

> Old TRSDOS diskettes to be used under the NEW TRSDOS MUST be XFERSYSed before use. Once XFERSYSed, an OLD TRSDOS diskette becomes a NEW TRSDOS diskette and should not be used with OLD TRSDOS again. If you started with an OLD system or data diskette, the XFERSYSed diskette will be a NEW system or data diskette respectively. OLD diskettes used under NEW TRSDOS without XFERSYSing, may cause extraneous information to be read at the end of files, giving a false End-of-File (EOF) indication.

I found an independently produced manual called *The TRS-80 Model III Users Guide* that rescued me with its clearly-written text, easy-to-understand examples, and well-drawn illustrations. Later, a new manual was issued with the TRS-80 Model 4P. Although it's a megastep ahead of the first one, it's still too technical for a beginner. I feel the best in the TRS series is the documentation for the TRS-80 Model 100 briefcase computer. One hopes computer companies are recognizing this weakness, and in the future documentation will be one of the best means of learning to use computers.

Can you try to learn too much? Definitely. I discovered early on that it was not necessary to understand the mechanical details of how the machine works. Unless you're a "nuts and bolts" person with particular interest in circuit boards and microchips, forget about the insides of the computer and concentrate on learning how to use one. They seem to be durable and need very little maintenance. Repairs are relatively easy to arrange, and it really isn't necessary to be an amateur engineer.

It is also unnecessary to master programming—that is writing a step-by-step procedure that allows the computer to perform a certain function. It helps to have some orientation in how computer languages such as BASIC are used to tell the computer what you want it to do. But you can buy programs already prepared for your particular machine. These programs are called software programs. While I've learned enough about programming to write a few procedures for my own use, mostly for fun, I'm convinced that I'll never, nor do I need to, become a computer programmer.

So as an educational goal, aim at a basic ability to use a microcomputer in your ministry. Take courage from the pilgrimage of a nonuser like me. With a fairly simple self-teaching technique I cut through the intimidating mystique of the computer world at least far enough to feel very much at home with my fingers on the keyboard and my eyes on the screen of my Model 4P.

According to Jeff Berner, Mark Twain was the first professional author to own a typewriter and probably the first to submit a typed manuscript (*The Adventures of Huckleberry Finn*) for publication. In 1874 he saw a Remington Model I in a Boston shop window, went inside for a demonstration, and bought it for $125. He never got the hang of using it, gave up after a few months, and went back to handwritten manuscripts. Years later, he joked that this was one of the two or three bloodless revolutions he had participated in.[2]

The cost of basic computer equipment today is comparably no greater than Mark Twain's investment in a Remington typewriter in 1874. Wouldn't it be a shame for a minister to make the same mistake Twain made, by refusing to employ a technique which could increase productivity many times over, especially when thousands of others in less significant vocations are risking the unfamiliarities of this "new-fangled Star Wars technology" and finding it enormously useful.

The following brief glossary may help to interpret computer lingo and give you a beginning vocabulary.

BASIC: A popular computer programming language that uses English-like statements. BASIC is an acronym for "Beginner's All-Purpose Symbolic Instruction Code."

Byte: Eight pieces of electronic or digital information. Most personal computers work with one byte of information at a time.

Compatible: Able to work together. Compatible software refers to software that can be used in a specific brand of computer without being changed. Compatible hardware is equipment that can be used together, such as a particular computer and a particular printer.

CPU: Abbreviation for "Central Processing Unit," the internal heart of the computer that handles most of the calculations. The term is often used interchangeably with the word *microprocessor.*

Data Storage: Data or information can be stored on audiocassettes when cassette players similar to standard audiocassette players are attached to the computer. Or data can be saved on floppy disks. About five inches in diameter, they look very much like a 45 RPM audio record, except that they are flexible. Disk players, or drives, are sometimes built into the computer or can be plugged in as an extra. Audiocassette storage is cheaper, but the disks provide far greater capacity and the quickest access to information. Most experts recommend disk storage if you can afford it.

Disk Drive: A device that may connect to the computer or may be built in. It lets the computer use floppy disks for storing programs or information.

Display: The television-like screen on which a computer displays the information. Some computers plug into a regular television set, but the special monitors that come with the computer will provide a sharper, easier to read display. If word processing will be a major use for the computer, a display screen with eighty characters per line and a total of twenty-four or twenty-five lines is best. Some machines have displays that can produce high-density graphic designs, graphs, and so forth. There are full-color displays available as well as black and white, green, and amber for less eyestrain.

Documentation: The written instructions that come with the computer or software.

Dot-Matrix Printer: A popular type of computer printer that prints characters by forming tiny dots on the paper.

Floppy Disk: Magnetic disk used for storing and recalling data or programs. The disk is flexible, hence the name.

Hardware: The physical parts of the computer, such as the keyboard, display monitor, disk drives, or central processing unit (CPU).

K: Abbreviation commonly used to describe the memory capacity of a computer. One K equals 1,000 bytes (pieces) of information.

Keyboard: Typewriter-style arrangement of keys for placing information into the computer. Most have number keys in the usual places as a typewriter keyboard and also a "numeric pad" with number keys arranged like an adding machine. There may also be "function keys" which save time by performing complicated operations by pushing one button.

Memory: The part of the computer that stores the information. It may be called storage.

Modem: Stands for Modulation/Demodulation. A device that allows computers to talk to each other over the telephone.

Program: A set of instructions that tells the computer the steps to perform.

Software: Sets of instructions called programs used to give directions to the mechanical parts of the computer.

Notes

1. John Naisbitt, *Megatrends* (New York: Warner Books, Inc., 1984), pp. 4-5.
2. Jeff Berner, *The Foolproof Guide to SCRIPSIT,* (Berkeley, Calif.: Sybex, 1983), p. xx.

2
Equipment and Programs

Any author who attempts to describe the current "state of the art" in computer hardware runs the risk of being out-of-date before his work is published. In fact it's more than a risk, it's a certainty; the computer field is changing rapidly and constantly. In the short time since I began writing this book, Radio Shack has introduced its "revolutionary" new Model 2000, Apple has premiered its "revolutionary" new Macintosh, and IBM has announced its "revolutionary" new Portable PC. And I'm only on chapter 2.

Before the book is ready for the publisher, there'll be more "revolutions" in the world of computers than in all the strife-torn countries of the world put together! To paraphrase the Book of Ecclesiastes, "Of the making of many word processors, there is no end."

Why do you laugh when you thumb through a 1930 edition of the Sears catalog? Because the merchandise looks so outdated and the prices are ridiculous. For the same reasons, it's just as funny to thumb through the pages of the article on "Computers" in our 1966 edition of *The World Book Encyclopedia.* Even though it's less than twenty years old, the article is so antiquated that its pictures and text are comical.

Further evidence of this accelerating advance is *Time* magazine's description of the Defense Department's giant computers installed in 1974. "Paleolithic" is what *Time* called these ten-year-old machines!

The growth of the computer industry is often called an

"explosion," and it really is! Who could have foreseen it? In 1948 the founder of IBM predicted that as many as *twelve companies* might someday have their own computers. Six years later it was obvious that estimate was too conservative, so in 1954 the prediction was boldly expanded to fifty companies. Experts aren't always expert at forecasting the future of technology.

I remember when *Popular Mechanics* predicted 500,000 homes with Picturephones by 1980. Do you have any neighbors with Picturephones? I also remember how for twenty-five years, banking has been "poised to leap into the cashless, checkless, electronic-money world." *Changing Times* lamented in 1968 that we would not see the end of checks until the mid-1970s.

In 1959 there were only 2,000 computers operating in the entire country. But by the end of 1983 there were thirteen million computers worldwide. The number doubled between 1981 and 1982 and doubled again between 1982 and 1983. In the twelve months of 1983 IBM shipped more personal computers than *all* the computers it had shipped up to 1983.[1]

Americans spent $10 billion on personal, desktop computers in 1983 alone. IBM led the top ten by selling $1.5 billion; Apple and Tandy tied for second place with about $1.1 billion in sales each. Still, only 7 percent of the office workers and 10 percent of the households in the U.S. had computers in 1983, so the personal computer industry is still in its infancy. By 1988 computer sales in the U.S. are expected to pass the $40 billion mark in one year.[2] More than four million college students will own a microcomputer by 1987, according to a study by Talmis, a computer-industry research firm.[3] It doesn't take an expert to predict that society eventually will be up to its microchips in computers.

With such explosive development, a writer's risk of being outdated is great. But it is not so great, if the writer discusses types or categories of computers. For within this shifting diversity some standardization has emerged, grouping certain kinds of computers together. So while it's risky to describe specific models as state of the art, it's fairly safe to talk about various classes of computer hardware without appearing dated.

Mainframe Computers

These are the giants, the megamachines, used primarily by government agencies, corporations, and institutions. In the 1940s, when the first electronic computers were built, they cost millions, and only world-class scientists were permitted to use them. The Smithsonian Institution's Museum of American History displays remnants of one such early giant, the ENIAC. A cumbersome, number-crunching computer built by the University of Pennsylvania in 1946, it weighed thirty tons, filled several rooms, and each day dozens of its 19,000 vacuum tubes had to be changed.

Then came the transistor and the microchip, making it possible for tiny hand-held calculators to have memory capacities and speed far greater than the "room-size monsters" of earlier years. Furthermore, microchip technology costs less, so computer prices plummeted.

It's no surprise then that in *The Third Wave* Alvin Toffler noted that if the auto industry had done what the computer industry has done in the last few years, a Rolls Royce would cost $2.50 and get 2,000,000 miles to the gallon![4]

There are still computers that cost millions of dollars and fill several floors of a building. Miniaturization has multiplied the capacity and speed of these new "Goliaths" until their vital statistics are incredible. Fans of George Orwell's *1984* get cold chills when they read about the IRS's vast computer network capable of monitoring minute details in the life of every American. But that's not a hypothetical Orwellian prediction; it's a fact.

Most modern mainframes, however, have more modest vital statistics. Used by businesses and institutions, they cost hundreds of thousands of dollars. Typically, the primary equipment fills several rooms, and a network of individual terminals connected to the mainframe allows numerous employees to use the machine simultaneously.

One handy example of the mainframe category is the IBM at Southwestern Seminary in Fort Worth. Terry Bratton, the director of the computer center, described it dramatically: "Squatting in the basement of B. H. Carroll Memorial Building, an IBM 4341 spreads its long, black, double-insulated tenacles of computerized efficiency through the campus at a rate that threatens to save money, cut time, and slash frustration in the paper mill."

Sounds ominous! Actually, it's a very friendly machine that operates our registration, library catalog, student and alumni records, and financial accounting procedures. Every second during the working day it handles 2.5 transactions from fifty-one terminals around the campus.

Students looking for a book in the seminary library no longer use a card catalog; they type in requests on one of sixteen computer terminals in the library, and in less than a second a complete list and location of every book in the 700,000-item collection by author, subject, or title flash on the screen.

Those of us who grew up with card files, and who belong to that generation of students who think of paper and pencil as holy objects, are a little intimidated by the new generation of library users. They step up so matter-of-factly to the terminals to find their books. They don't even have to refer to the printed directions. Punching computer keys is natural to them.

There are times when I long for the good old days of light oak cabinets with labeled 3 x 5 drawers through which you could browse in search of material. Who hasn't relished that momentary flush of autonomy knowing you could even remove the drawer completely to a nearby table, and have it all to yourself while you flipped undisturbed through its contents? I still get nostalgic when I see small scraps of paper or little golf pencils like those the librarian always kept on the catalog tables for your notes. But those days are gone forever.

Now the catalog is "on-line," accessible only to the technologically initiated. Admittedly, once you've taken the computer plunge (or been dragged into it kicking and screaming), you begin to enjoy the advantages, such as the instant report of a book's availability and the faster circulation procedures. A computer scanner reads the student's ID number and the code on the book's cover and checks it out automatically while deleting the title from the available list. It instantly "tattles" to the librarian if the student owes a fine or has an overdue book. An alarm sounds if the patron accidently exits the library without checking out the book. Of course, in our seminary, that never happens. Well, at least it seldom happens. Anyway, the computer is prepared to handle such rare situations.

Southwestern's mainframe quickly moves students through registration in just forty-five minutes and maintains an updated record of grades, courses taken, progress toward their degree, and courses remaining to complete their work. Bratton says of those who work with him in the Computer Center, "The exciting thing is that the Lord keeps sending us students who are highly qualified professionals, and that lets us do so much toward improving the efficiency of the seminary operations."

The seminary computer is a typical example of the mainframe—obviously not a category you will try to use in personal ministry.

Minicomputers

Small desktop computers, called minicomputers, cost from $10,000 to $100,000 because of sophisticated features that make them especially applicable for heavy business use. While they look like a personal computer, "minis" are more complex and powerful. With their large memory capacities and business software programs, they can handle with efficiency the accounting, word processing, personnel records, tax calculations, and mailing lists of a major organization. Furthermore, through networking (connecting a number of computers together), the simple "mini" can be converted into a system to serve a number of offices within the organization. Because they provide more than you'll need, it would be technological "overkill" to choose a minicomputer for your ministerial use.

Microcomputers or Personal Computers

Arriving on the scene only recently, microcomputers have revolutionized the industry. Also known as personal computers, they generally cost between $1000 and $10,000, and are sold under such popular brands as Apple, IBM, Radio Shack, and others. Although the prices of some microcomputers have fallen below $1,000, most systems—including computer, disk drives, modem, and printer—cost between $2,000 and $4,000.

Since the micro or personal computer is the one you're most likely to use as a pastor or church staff member, let's take a closer look at the one I'm using as a typical example. It's a TRS-80 Model 4P by Radio Shack. The "P" indicates it is the portable version of the Model 4 desktop computer. I have grouped portable computers in a separate category, but since mine also functions as a regular desktop micro, I will tell about it here.

The computer itself, consisting of the central processing unit, display screen, and two 5 1/4" floppy disk drives, is contained in a single unit, 16 x 13 x 10 inches. (Now might be a good time to refer again to the glossary in chapter 1 for definitions of terms.) Unlike the sterile gray of earlier TRS models, the case is an attractive off-white plastic with black trim. The power cord and cable connections are concealed behind a closed compartment, so it even looks handsome from the rear!

The display screen measures 9" diagonally and, in technical

computerese, has a "high resolution 80 x 24 display." That means its letters, numbers, and symbols are clearly displayed, and that there are twenty-four lines of text with eighty characters in each line. That's a minimum standard for quality machines and is adequate for any application you'll need, including word processing. Even though it is considerably smaller than the standard 12" monitor of a regular desktop computer, the 9" screen is easy to read. Portability and smaller desk space are justifiable trade-offs for the larger screen.

The Model 4P has 64K internal memory, which, with a little extra cash, can be expanded to 128K. Each of its two storage disks holds 180,000 characters, and additional drives can be added for still more storage. I've used the Model 4P for a year now, and have gotten along well without the extra internal memory and disk drives.

Attached to the unit by a 15" cord is a full-size typewriter keyboard that I can use on my lap or at adjustable angles on my desk. In addition to the regular keys, it has a 12-key numeric keypad like those on an adding machine.

Scores of TRS software programs will run on the Model 4P, as will programs in the popular CP/M format. To operate CP/M programs (such as IBM software), you have to buy CP/M disks that load into the machine first. What all this means is that I have more software programs available than I could ever use.

Connected to my computer by a thin cable is a TRS Daisy Wheel Printer (the DWP 210). Its black and off-white matching case measures 6 x 20 x 13 inches. At a speed of over two hundred words a minute, it produces "letter-quality" copies of anything on the computer screen or in its memory. Another thin cable connects a modem, which is itself connected to a telephone line. This allows me to dial up any of the numerous data banks and information services around the country.

If I need to take the computer on a trip, I slide the keyboard into its storage compartment, unplug the printer and modem, and wind up the power cord in its designated track. Then I snap on the cover, grab the whole thing by its built-in disappearing handle, and go. It only weighs twenty-six pounds. Can you imagine the convenience of taking such a powerful tool with you to that cabin in the mountains for a week of sermon preparation or book writing? If only I had a cabin in the mountains!

Unintentionally, the preceding paragraphs sound like advertising copy for Radio Shack hardware. But they're not. I do like my setup, but computer users' tastes vary. The proud owners of an IBM PC or an Apple IIe, for example, are as loyal to their equipment as I am to mine. To each his own. My excuse for waxing eloquent about my equipment is that it is typical of this category. Whichever microcomputer you fall in love with and purchase will be very much like the TRS-80 I've fondly described.

Home Computers

Several inexpensive computers are on the market in this category, some for less than $100. For the most part, they're designed for entertainment and educational programs, but some can perform simple home management procedures as well. The home model is OK as a starter, but it won't be satisfactory for the purposes of your work as a minister.

Portable Computers

Another recent advance in computer hardware is the portable unit, which folds up to about the size of a sixteen-millimeter movie projector or a large portable typewriter. Sometimes the term *transportable* is used and is more accurate, since some weigh as much as fifty pounds. While the display screen will be smaller, it will usually have the same capacity as a full-size microcomputer. The portable will perform all the functions of the regular machine, including word processing. While some models will have additional features such as built-in modems and software programs, most will be similar to my TRS-80 Model 4P.

Briefcase Computers

Often referred to as "notebook computers," these baby units are remarkably powerful and efficient. Mine is a TRS-80 Model 100, about the size of a typical three-ring notebook. In spite of its tiny dimensions, it has a full-size typewriter keyboard, a small display screen with eight forty-character lines, 32K memory, and five built-in programs. Not only will it do an acceptable job of word processing, but has address file, calendar schedule, and telecommunications programs as well. It uses Microsoft BASIC as a language, and with a self-contained modem for telephone communications, it can log on to remote data banks.

Since it is powered by flashlight batteries as well as an AC power cord, the briefcase computer can be used anywhere. Some airline companies restrict the use of portable electronic equipment, but I composed portions of this book using the Model 100 in an airliner at 40,000 feet! That still gets attention even in our sophisticated, technologically jaded age.

Just think, from a remote location, even a motel room in a distant city, I can plug the Model 100 into a telephone, call the seminary and receive on the miniature screen the entire library catalog, student records, and other information from the IBM mainframe. Or I can call CompuServe information service and receive articles from the *Washington Post,* airline schedules, any article in an electronic encyclopedia, and more. Unbelievable! We'll enlarge on getting information from data banks in a later chapter.

Recently, in an Executive Committee meeting in Nashville, I heard the familiar quiet clicking of a Model 100 keyboard. I glanced around, and there he was—a news editor on the row behind me, taking notes on his briefcase computer. What flexibility! No wonder institutions such as Dallas Baptist College are requiring entering students to purchase the TRS-80

Model 100 when they register. The cost is included in their fees, so it belongs to them when they finish their degrees.

Swept along by the public's accelerating demand for the new and different, other manufacturers are bringing out their own briefcase models—each a little smaller, lighter, and more efficient (and usually more expensive) than the previous models. Seiko now sells a wristwatch computer with 2K of memory!

You could begin your computer orientation with a briefcase unit, but they're not sufficient for the full range of ministry tasks. Ideally, if you can afford both, a briefcase computer and a desktop unit work well in tandem. For example, you could transfer from your Model 4 to your Model 100 certain prospect or membership records, take the portable with you when you visit, and in your car call up on its little screen other names in the zip code area where you happen to be at the time. The chapter on personal visitation will enlarge on this application for the minister.

Even though earlier I said the risk of being outdated is not as great when you talk about categories as when you talk about specific hardware, I still have a lingering apprehension that by the time you read this section it will seem pathetically outdated. The exclamation points I've inserted to express my amazement at the latest new devices will probably amuse you. I can understand that.

It reminds me of the letter I wrote my parents in 1951 when I was a senior at Baylor University:

> Tell Don [my little brother] he should see the new drink machines just installed in Brooks Hall. You put in a quarter, select your drink, a cup drops into place and fills up, and the machine even gives you your change automatically!!!!!!!

Notice the number of exclamation points. I was really impressed. Well, I'm equally amazed at the dazzling advancements being made in modern computers. And having gushed about them on these pages, in years to come comments are certain to resemble my old college letter. But at least I've restrained my use of exclamation points; there are only a few and so far I've not put in more than one at a time!

Computer Software

Since the purpose of this chapter is to give you an overview of the computer resources available for your use in ministry, it will be necessary to talk about programs as well as machines. You'll remember from the glossary in chapter 1 that software and program are interchangeable terms. A program is a set of instructions that tells the computer how to perform the task you give it. Suppose you want to use your computer to do word processing, that is, writing text for a sermon or an article. It's possible to turn on the machine according to the instruction manual and begin typing words that will appear on the screen. But that's all.

You can't indent paragraphs, set line spacing, move blocks of text, delete or add material, set margins and tabs, save the material for later use, or any of the essential functions of writing. To do those things you need a program.

If you know how to program a computer yourself, you can send it instructions directly by typing them on the keyboard. But in order to do that, you have to learn a special language. My Model 4P's programming language is called BASIC. There are others such as FORTRAN, COBOL, LOGO, and PILOT, but BASIC is the most popular for microcomputers. It uses a set of codes and instructions which the machine understands.

At times instructions written in BASIC sound almost like regular English:

CLS: PRINT "THE SQUARE ROOT OF 2 IS" SQR(2).

If you type this simple program into the computer and press the "enter" key, it will immediately run your program and give you the answer:

THE SQUARE ROOT OF 2 IS 1.41421.

Sounds simple. But it's not. BASIC has a complex system of syntax and protocol and a weird vocabulary: GOTO, HIMEM, BLOAD, MID$, GOSUB, TROFF, PEEK, POKE, CHR$. Furthermore, a relatively simple program in BASIC requires several lines of instructions written with unforgiving precision. Here's an example of a simple program to determine if a number is odd or even.

```
10 REM THIS PROGRAM DETERMINES IF A NUM-
BER IS ODD OR EVEN
20 PRINT "INPUT NUMBER"
30 INPUT N
40 Y = N/2 − INT (N/2)
50 IF Y 0 THEN 80
60 PRINT "THE NUMBER IS EVEN"
70 GOTO 90
80 PRINT "THE NUMBER IS ODD"
90 END
```

Type in these instructions exactly as they're printed, and if your computer speaks BASIC, when you ask it to run the program, it will follow the steps line by line. A message will appear on the screen asking you to type in a number, any number. Push the "enter" key, and immediately the screen will respond with "the number is odd" or "the number is even."

Yes, I know it's easier just to look at a number's last digit, to determine whether it's odd or even. I also know that any number divisible by 2 is an even number, but I've learned that authors of computer books use this kind of illustration all the time. So just go along with me this time, and accept it as an example of a simple program you can write yourself.

A complex program such as the word processor I'm using requires hundreds of lines, involving tangled BASIC syntax. Just to copy it precisely would require hours of tedious work.

To go further and learn how to create an original word processing program would require a major course in programming. Early on in my brief computer experience, I claimed the right never to be a programmer. I also determined there was no need to be, since I can buy ready-made programs on a disk or a cassette tape.

Although the Model 4P will run what is called CP/M software, most programs I use are manufactured by Radio Shack exclusively for their machines. Other computer brands usually do the same: IBM programs run on IBM computers, and Apple programs run on Apples.

Isn't there some standardization that will allow all programs to work on all machines, like cassettes work on all cassette recorders? Not yet, but gradually it's emerging. Some say IBM will be the standard of the future. So more and more manufacturers are producing "IBM-Clones" and "IBM-compatible" programs. Others vote for CP/M, still others for MS-DOS, and recently a system called UNIX has gained popularity as the future generic operating system. This emerging standardization, even though far from developed, means that already there are hundreds of programs for sale that will work on most popular computers.

Your main concern is to find the programs you're most likely to use and then be certain the computer you buy will run them. Get almost any copy of a good computer magazine and turn to the "Software Review" section. There will always be one. I know from browsing through most of them. In that section you will find presented the strengths and weaknesses of programs—sometimes with charts comparing features and prices. You can shop for programs in the computer stores too, but, unfortunately, salespersons are seldom able to tell as much as the magazine articles.

In chapter 1, I listed five computer applications you would most likely use: word processing, filing, financial planning, accessing data bases, and family educational and entertainment programs. Software is changing as rapidly as hardware, but a brief review of some popular programs in each of these categories may help.

Word Processing Programs

They range from very simple, inexpensive programs with limited features to complex giants that can do everything. Somewhere in between the extremes of very simple and complex giants is the program I'm using to write this book.

SuperSCRIPSIT is its name. It comes on a paper-thin 5 1/4" floppy disk accompanied by 300 pages of instructions and four cassette learning tapes. When I slide the disk inside the disk drive (that's the slot in the computer that looks like a toaster, remember?), push the reset button, and type in the word *SCRIPSIT,* the program "loads" into the computer. I don't understand where in the innards of my machine it lodges (or even where they get a funny name like SuperSCRIPSIT), but after all the whirring and humming ends, the screen comes alive. It welcomes me to a writing session by politely offering a list of options:

(O) OPEN A DOCUMENT
(D) DISPLAY DISK DIRECTORY
(S) SYSTEM SETUP UTILITY
(P) PROOFREAD A DOCUMENT
(C) COMPRESS A DOCUMENT
(A) ASCII TEXT CONVERSION UTILITY
(E) EXIT TO TRSDOS

WHAT IS YOUR SELECTION?

Now don't worry if you can't understand all those options. Selection (E) sounds like a sign on the interstate. (C) sounds suspicious. Could it be a method for shortening lengthy sermons? Or does it print your document in diminutive letters? No. Actually, it's a way the program stores your writing on a disk in the least amount of space possible. But you don't have to know that now.

Neither do you have to know what option (A) means. Does it convert your sermon text from KJV TO RSV? Or is it a utilitarian method for finding good sermon texts on "conversion" such as John 3:16? Neither. It's just a process to change your floppy disks from one format to another so they can be used on different computers. (Take heart. You'll soon get so used to all this jargon that you won't laugh every time you see the term *floppy disk.*)

Even though they may seem complicated, the features of SuperSCRIPSIT can be learned easily from the manuals, the cassettes, or a Radio Shack seminar. For now just be assured that if I can learn to use it, so can you. With a little practice, it will become natural—like riding a bicycle. (Somehow you knew I was going to say that, didn't you?)

Another word processing program being advertised in the magazines must surely be in the complex giant category. It packages several related programs under the brand, PROMPTDOC. Here's a tool that literally prompts you to write. By asking a series of questions about the subject, it draws even reluctant writers into the task. Think what that means for a writer who just can't get started. Little by little, the program builds your outline for you, then feeds it back to you for fleshing out. You're urged to write; text has to appear on the screen; sentences have to flow; words must be typed. Relentlessly, PROMPTDOC cajoles you to complete your entire project.

Next, there's a built-in electronic thesaurus. Suppose in the midst of your writing, you use a favorite, shopworn cliche. You know better. Use a cliche too often, and it becomes a shopworn cliche. You need, in the place of your shopworn cliche, a synonym that is not a cliche. No problem. Just press the "escape" key twice, and presto! A window appears on your screen filled with dozens of synonyms for your shopworn cliche. Choose the one you like, press "escape" again, and it replaces the shopworn cliche. The text opens or closes to accept the new word, and the screen looks as it did before, except your shopworn cliche has now become a scintilating gem of a word. (It's obvious from this paragraph that my word processor does *not* provide an automatic thesaurus.)

When you've finished writing, PROMPTDOC will check your document for spelling, punctuation, and grammar errors; either correcting mistakes automatically, or calling each infraction to your attention so you may correct it yourself. There is also a "Word-frequency Analyzer." It quickly sorts the words in your text by frequency. Thus you find you have used "thus" too often, so turn on the handy electronic thesaurus and replace a few "thuses" from its alternate vocabulary.

Is that all? Not a chance. This word processor has its own reputation on the line and isn't about to let you sully it with inappropriate phrases or sloppy literary style. It has a list of trite, clumsy, redundant, muddy, and wordy phrases that often appear in the work of amateur writers. Using this intimidating list as a guide, the computer scans your work and reminds you, for instance, that "a number of" is wordy and could be replaced by "many."

Now that's a word processor! Of course it's a deluxe model —in a class all by itself—and the price is consistent: currently more than $1,300.

Most word processors are not that expensive or multitalented. You can get a number of them for under $100 that will perform all the functions you'll need for writing sermons, books, or simple memos. (If I were using PROMPTDOC, I suppose it would have shamed me into saying: "you can get *many* of them. . . . ") Once you learn to use your word processor, you're spoiled. The chapter entitled "The Computer and Preaching" will go into greater detail about how helpful word processing can be in sermon preparation.

Filing Programs

One of the computer's most valuable skills is managing files—filing data by various categories and allowing its recall in any order. File your recipes and menus in the computer, for example. Then examine the leftovers in your refrigerator, listing to the computer those you can still identify by name. The filing program will retrieve all the recipes and menus that mention leftovers. Choose one, and you'll convince your family that you're some kind of technological gourmet.

PFS:FILE is a TRS-80 Model 4 filing program. The ads call it: "An easy-to-use personal filing program that works like a paper filing system, but without paper!" Maybe that's a little overstated, but it is simple and practical. You can decide how your records are to appear by organizing your information on "forms" you design right on the screen. The forms can have as much or as little structure as you wish.

Once you've created the basic form, just fill in the blanks, and enter them into the computer's memory. Regardless of the order in which you entered the information, you can retrieve it by whatever categories or in whatever order you like. And it takes only a fraction of the time it would take with a conventional filing system.

You can already see how this capability could enhance your work as a minister: membership records, evangelistic prospects, counseling information, sermon files, illustration files, music repertoires—the possibilities are numerous. Many of them will be presented later in the book.

A similar program I've used is PROFILE III PLUS. It will process more individual records than PFS:FILE, but with fewer data in each record. With two disk drives, you can work with 700 records of 255 characters in length. Add two additional drives and the capacity climbs to 2,100 records. The program allows you to print custom reports using the data, or you can merge PROFILE III PLUS with SuperSCRIPSIT and write form letters to selected persons on a mailing list.

Second generation filing programs are being marketed called "data-base management" programs. They do essentially the same tasks PFS:FILE and PROFILE III PLUS, but with expanded capacities, faster speeds, and extra features.

But beware of computer overkill. For many operations,

microcomputers are clearly inferior to simpler and less expensive devices, such as fingers and 3 x 5 cards. Maybe you've heard of the preacher who bought a $5000 IBM PC which he used primarily to keep track of his neckties. He could tell at a glance how many striped, patterned, and solid colors he had, what each had cost, when they were last cleaned and how many Sundays he had worn each one. There's nothing wrong with this. It just seems an extravagant use of sophisticated equipment for a trivial purpose. You don't need to buy a $10,000 solid gold sledgehammer to drive in a two-cent thumbtack.

Financial Planning Programs

Usually sold under the heading of Spreadsheets, these programs create columns and rows of information similar to accounting ledgers. Computer spreadsheets, however, have enormous capacities—over a hundred rows and columns can be created. You would have to use billboard-size ledger sheets to match them.

How can you get all those columns and rows on a 9" computer screen? I'm glad you asked. You simply push keys on the keyboard and the perpendicular columns scroll across the screen: A through Z, then AA through ZZ, then AAA through ZZZ, then AB through ZB, then—well, you get the picture. The horizontal rows scroll the same way, up and down, from Row 1 to the limit of your particular program. Key strokes also let you move quickly to a specific intersection of a column and row. For example, ask the computer to take you immediately to "Column RR, Row 395," and it obeys quicker than a flash.

At each intersection of a row and a column, you can enter a number, a name, or a mathematical formula. For instance, row 12 in column D can be a formula that always gives you the sum of the previous eleven rows of column D. Make any change in a figure in column D, and the sum in row 12D will automatically be updated. In fact, the entire spreadsheet, no matter how complex, will automatically adjust whenever you make a single change. A penciled spreadsheet on a yellow columnar pad works all right, but one error or change, and you'll wear out a dozen erasers correcting each column and row affected. The electronic spreadsheet does it immediately.

Furthermore, it's easier to work "what-if" problems and to do financial forecasts on the computer spreadsheet. Planning a budget, monitoring expenditures and cash flow, projecting enrollments under certain conditions—these are only a few of many applications.

A TRS version called VisiCalc allows me to plot the formula for funding the seminaries through the Southern Baptist Cooperative Program. All the factors can be applied in such a way that I can predict what would happen if: Southern Seminary's enrollment should go up 10 percent, New Orleans's down 5 percent, Southwestern's and the others' remain level, while the Cooperative Program budget increases by three million dollars.

VisiCalc and similar spreadsheet programs are powerful tools for financial planning, but there are other financial planning programs that are cheaper and easier to operate. One of the many simpler budget management, checkbook, or tax calculation programs which are abundantly available may be all you'll need.

Communication Programs

Most microcomputers have the capacity to communicate over telephone lines with other microcomputers or with distant data bases and information services. Sometimes the computer itself will have a built-in program for this purpose; others use packaged software which you load into the machine. The Model 4P has all the necessary features to communicate with a range of other micros through direct cable connections. Therefore, my briefcase Model 100 can exchange data with the Model 4P when I link them together with a cable.

But connect your computer to a modem, and, in turn, connect the modem to a telephone line, and you can "talk to" major data networks around the country such as CompuSERVE or THE SOURCE. There is usually a subscription charge and an inexpensive hourly rate for their use, but they place at your fingertips an incredible menu of information. Medical facts, weather, movie reviews, airline schedules, news, encyclopedia articles, bibliographies, to name only a fraction of the list.

STARTEXT is a local information service run by the *Fort Worth Star-Telegram* offering news, stock quotes, weather, the latest classifieds, all constantly updated. Just dial the number, listen for that distinctive tone that tells you the other computer has answered, touch the "control c" key, and the screen will welcome you, asking for your membership number and password. If all is in order, you will then be presented with a menu of topics, and you're ready to read and/or store the information you want.

Most national networks offer electronic mail services too. Leave a message for another subscriber, and the minute he logs on, he is notified that he has mail waiting. He calls for it and reads your message on his own screen.

Access to the growing number of these data bases offers a rich mine of research information for sermon preparation and other ministry tasks. We will explore that application later.

Family Programs

According to surveys, the most frequent use of a microcomputer in a home is playing electronic games. Since our children are grown, my TRS-80 is never—well, seldom—used for games. In part, that's because we also have other equipment connected to the television that plays games better than the computer.

Many of us have learned to play several video games on the television set, but maybe you didn't realize that, using the keyboard or a "joystick" accessory, the same games can be played on a microcomputer. Moreover, when you're playing, people assume you're hard at work on a serious computer project.

Computer games don't measure up to the quality of television games, however, unless you have a color monitor, sound capabilities, and a high-resolution monitor. These are expensive add-ons, difficult to justify; and you'll find your family probably enjoys the television variety better. If you're still interested, Radio Shack sells several computer games on floppy disks and cassettes for about the same price as the video versions. "Adventure" or "lost treasure" games play well on computers, and so do "mental" games such as acrostics, crossword puzzles, chess, backgammon, scrabble, and simulations.

On the other hand, the computer really shines when you use it for family educational purposes. K-8 MATH PROGRAM, VOL. I is a sample of many educational software programs. It randomly generates drill-and-practice problems in number concepts, addition, subtraction, multiplication, and division. There are built-in tests, and automatic promotion and demotion.

You can buy similar programs (or occasionally, they can be checked out at the library) for geometry, calculus, chemistry, physics, astronomy, reading, history, language arts, foreign languages—you name it. It's almost like having a complete public school curriculum on disks. Of course, you'll also find a number of programs on how to learn about computers.

Obviously, one of the valuable side benefits of having a microcomputer at home is the exposure family members can have to this exploding technology. Since computers will pervade every area of their lives, regardless of what God calls them to do, I would want my children to learn computer skills early. The microcomputer is a wise investment. It isn't often that an appliance so useful in vocational ministry can be, at the same time, so practical for family education and entertainment.

Where are computers headed? I'm no prophet, but here are some areas to watch.

Smaller and more sophisticated models. Notebook computers will get better and continue to be hot sellers. Computers that use, in addition to a keyboard, alternate input devices will grow in popularity too. Already there are machines you operate by touching the screen, by giving voice commands, or by moving the cursor with a small box on wheels called a "mouse."

Integrated software is one software program that combines many functions. For example, a spreadsheet, record-filer, word processor all in one. Another trend in the next few years will be the preloading of popular software programs into the computer and including them in its price.

Transactional services. Information services and data banks will allow you to do your banking and shopping, make airline reservations, or buy concert tickets without leaving home.

Friendlier operation. I remember the first salesman I consulted about computers. He tried to encourage me by saying, "This model is designed to be user-friendly." It did encourage me. I certainly didn't want a machine that was user-hostile or even user-indifferent. In the style of an intellectual name-dropper, he said his computer was a good example of "ergonomics"—the science of trying to improve the environment in which people work. I'd never heard of ergonomics, and even now it isn't a word I use every day. Still, it was comforting to know that the term exists, and that computer companies are striving to make their products easier and friendlier to operate.

This morning, in fact, the *Today Show* featured a new computerized "chalkboard" as an illustration of this simplification. Even though they lacked the manual dexterity normally required to operate a computer keyboard, two five-year-olds were able to perform complex operations on a computer by moving their fingers across an "electronic slate," or chalkboard. No one can accurately predict what's ahead for computers, but these trends, already emerging, will surely continue.

As the authors of *Naked Computer* point out, "No nook, no cranny of society will be spared the invasion of computers. But weep not. The little devils seem benign. Almost friendly, even."[5] If, up until now, you've been suffering from a bad case of computer phobia, now might be a good time to take the first step into this friendly new world.

Notes

1. Information about the computer boom is from John Bear, *The Computer Wimp* (Berkeley, Calif.: Ten Speed Press, 1983), pp. 8-9; Anna Mae Burke, *The Plain Brown Wrapper Book of Computers* (San Francisco: Harbor Publishing Co., 1983), p. 22; Gerry Barker, "Computer Mania," *Fort Worth Magazine,* April 1984, pp. 8-12.
2. "1983 Grand Totals," *80 Micro,* February 1984, p. 34.
3. *Chronicle of Higher Education,* May 23, 1984, p. 13.
4. See Barker, p. 8.
5. Quoted in Barker, p. 12. The authors of *Naked Computer* are Jack B. Rochester and John Gantz.

3
The Personal Computer and Preaching

Before becoming president of the seminary, I helped organize an informal meeting for pastors of large metropolitan churches. Three days each year, we gathered to share experiences and ideas, in what became for us one of the most valuable meetings on the calendar. At the first meeting in Callaway Gardens, Georgia, each preacher told how he usually prepared sermons. I was amazed. Each pastor's style was different, and the differences were radical. Several of the preachers planned so far ahead they had Easter sermons completed by December! Others organized their work so that Sunday morning's sermon was always ready by Wednesday, and Sunday evening's message by Friday. At the opposite end of this ministerial spectrum, was one preacher who worked on his sermon through the week, but always waited until Sunday morning to write it out. I'd be a nervous wreck if I waited until early Sunday morning to finish my sermon; but for him it was a system that worked well. Two things were clear from that meeting: first, there are as many sermon preparation styles as there are preachers, and, second, my style wasn't so bad after all!

As a pastor, you have no task more important than preaching. There may be other pastoral duties you enjoy more, but the primary responsibility to which God has called you is preparing and delivering sermons. Each Lord's Day you stand in the pulpit before a congregation expecting to hear a word from God. Their minds are preoccupied with questions that are deeper than life, and they want answers. Some are worried about important decisions they must make next week, decisions that will affect their lives and the lives of their families. They need guidance. Heartbroken and pressured, they bring with them guilt, anxiety, and discouragement, and they want to be reassured that God will help them.

And there you stand, every eye fixed on you, every ear listening. What a responsibility! You dare not take it lightly. You must not step to that pulpit unprepared. They'll not be helped by a shallow presentation of your opinions; they're waiting for the Word of God. You may be proud of your sense of humor, but they're not here to be entertained, no matter how clever you are. Don't try to dazzle them with a brilliant analysis of some favorite theological trivia. They want spiritual encouragement, assurance, forgiveness, and strength, and it's up to you to help them find it in God's Word. Can you imagine any task more challenging?

On the other hand, there is no task more exciting, more fulfilling than the preparation and delivery of sermons. The times I've felt closest to the Lord during my thirty-two years of ministry have been in the study with the open Bible before me on the desk, or in the sanctuary with the open Bible before me on the pulpit. Often, at my desk, an insight would flash into my consciousness as if a light switch had been turned on. An illustration that was just right would come to mind. Or, halfway through a familiar verse I had read a hundred times, there would emerge some exciting new meaning. Gushing with enthusiasm, I would rush from the study to show Betty my new insight, only to be reminded that these mystical moments were really meant to encourage me at a particular time. I couldn't express them to her in the same way. You just had to be there.

Furthermore, there were those exquisite moments when I sensed in the midst of preaching a sermon that it really was happening. God really was speaking through the sermon! Those are the mountain peaks in a preacher's life. You've been there, and you know what I mean. So, let's examine that challenging and exciting duty you face every week in the pastoral ministry: preparing sermons.

The Computer and Sermon Preparation

Your personal style of preparing sermons may be unique. It may not be a classic style that homiletics experts would applaud, but it's your style. Sure, it could use some improvements, but it works pretty well, and you have no great urge to change it. My purpose here is not to discuss the merits of various methods of sermon preparation, but to show how the computer can enhance and improve whatever system you use.

Every style, no matter how unique, will include, in some order, each of the following steps.

1. Prayerfully choosing a text or subject for your sermon.
2. Thoroughly exegeting the biblical material to determine what the text meant in its original historical context.
3. Honestly interpreting the text to determine what it means to the people who will hear your sermon.
4. Carefully developing a thesis and an outline of your sermon.
5. Completely writing out your sermon in a manuscript or a detailed outline.
6. Sufficiently rehearsing your sermon in order to preach it confidently.
7. Faithfully preserving your sermon material in a file for future use.
8. Hopefully, preaching your sermon again on other occasions in the future.

This natural cycle of sermon preparation, delivery, and filing is essential to good homiletics. You can shortcut the cycle, but the quality of preparation and, therefore, the effectiveness of the sermon will suffer. Since all the elements are important, you should organize your time schedule, library resources, office personnel, and devotional time to allow the complete cycle to function each week.

Can a microcomputer help you with this recurring cycle? Yes. Looking back, I wish the computer had been available to help me prepare and store those 2,000 sermons filed in the shelves behind my desk. OK, so I was born thirty years too soon. But I'm catching up fast, and in just a short time, I've learned to apply computer skills to many of the routine responsibilities of my work, including the steps of sermon preparation. Here are some suggestions that may help you take the electronic plunge, too.

Choosing a Text or a Subject

While the computer may not give great assistance in this important step, it does put you in touch with some clever tools to make it easier. One is an ingenious program marketed by Bible Research Systems in Austin, Texas, called THE WORD Processor. It's an electronic concordance of the King James Version of the Bible. Load it into your computer, and you can search both the Old and New Testaments for words, phrases, or names, and set up your own indexed files for personal study. The company has just released an added feature that lets you search the Bible for topics, too. For example, you can automatically list on your screen or on your printer all the passages dealing with "Spiritual Gifts," "Doubt," "Hope," "Fellowship with Christ," or more than 200 other topics.

THE WORD Processor can help you find that passage from God's Word you need as a text or a scriptural background for your subject. I predict there will soon be a flood of similar programs on the market, and, if the usual pattern of software development is repeated, each one will be better than the last. You'll be glad you have the equipment to use them.

Exegesis and Interpretation

Having easy access to commentaries and books for sermon preparation is one of the great advantages of living in the Fort

Worth area. Our chamber of commerce may not list that advantage in its brochures, but it's important to us preachers who live here. We have access to the largest theological library in the United States, the A. Webb Roberts Library at Southwestern Seminary. Not only is it large, it's also technologically ahead of its time. Recently, when we moved the library to its new facilities, we electronically recorded the card catalog in the memory of our huge mainframe computer. Now, library patrons search the catalog by typing their requests on any of the fifty computer terminals scattered across the campus.

Sure, that's a great help to those who live near the seminary, but what if you're pastor of the Antelope Baptist Church or the First Baptist Church in Clifton, miles away from the campus? Have no fear. The marvel of computer technology is about to come to your rescue. It's now possible to access our entire library card catalog remotely, using the keyboard of a personal computer, even from Antelope or Clifton. A few months ago, we installed, on an experimental basis, the equipment to make this possible.

A Gandalf Unit (don't ask me to explain what that is or how it got its name) is connected to the seminary mainframe. It causes our IBM 4341 to exchange information with your micro just as it would with one of its own 3,278 terminals. If your computer is connected to the seminary computer by telephone, then you can type instructions on your keyboard, and the big computer in our basement thinks it's talking with a terminal on campus. (You can't fool mother nature, but you *can* fool an IBM 4341.)

Here's how it works. Sitting at my desk at home, I load a software program called TELETERM-EM into my disk drive. The screen offers me four options, including the one that allows me to connect my TRS-80 Model 4P to Southwestern's IBM 4341. I choose that option, and when prompted, type in "VT100," the kind of terminal I want to emulate, and then I'm ready to make the connection. It sounds complicated, but the instructions clearly lead you through each step. Next, I dial the special seminary computer number (by long distance, if necessary), activate my modem when the tone tells me the seminary computer has answered, type in the proper passwords, and presto! the screen says, "Welcome to Southwestern Seminary." I request the library catalog, and from then on have access to the same research information I would have if I were standing in the lobby of the library itself.

This new system allows you, wherever you live, to touch the keys on your own keyboard and look through the catalog to find the commentaries and other material that will help you prepare your sermon. In a few days the books you need can be delivered to your door because Southwestern even has a procedure for checking them out to you by mail. (Membership in the library's Continuing Education Program is required. For a modest enrollment fee, individuals may join this program.)

The capability to make the electronic catalog available is in place now, but we are still experimenting with the procedures, and when they are perfected we will offer the service to pastors. We will also develop a theological and biblical data base similar to other information services around the country. Soon you will be able to log on to STABIS (Southwestern Theological and Biblical Information Service) and transfer directly to your personal computer information on a variety of relevant subjects.

But you don't have to wait for STABIS. Already, massive amounts of information for sermon research are available to the computer-equipped pastor. General information services such as CompuServe offer on-line encyclopedia articles, news events, health facts, and data on hundreds of current subjects, all instantly available right at your desk.

Browsing through their computer section during one of my recent forays to a local bookstore, I discovered a 500-page volume entitled *The Computer Phone Book.*[1] It listed over four hundred bulletin boards, information services, and other networks you can access with your microcomputer. The variety of subjects listed is almost endless: dating services, advertising, health, games, space, sororities, want ads, self-help programs, role-playing, counseling, alternate energy sources, dial-a-joke, and the list goes on. Regretfully, but not surprising in our permissive society, some of the bulletin boards specialize in sexually explicit material. Satan already is at work in this infant industry.

There is, however, a brighter side. I've found many bulletin boards which have a Christian orientation. "Computers for Christ" in Ontario, California, is one of several listed in *The Phone Book.* Its special purpose, according to the listing, is to provide "text files on various religious subjects, with special emphasis on Christianity." Mike Cane, the author of the directory, said, "I would like to note that one of the high points in compiling *The Computer Phone Book* was having an on-line chat with the sysop of this BBS."[1] (Sysop means system operator, and BBS stands for Bulletin Board Service.) Mike Cane was obviously touched by the witness of this Christian technician. Thankfully, the Holy Spirit also is at work in this infant industry.

I hope a creative Christian computer expert will soon find a way to penetrate these mushrooming national networks for the purpose of "on-line evangelism." But that's a subject for another book. The point here is that the preacher has a huge treasure of information for sermon research right at his fingertips.

One of the national networks, for example, is BRS AFTER DARK, a new venture of Bibliographic Retrieval Service (BRS), a company that has primarily provided databases to businesses, universities, and libraries. BRS has been expensive, but BRS AFTER DARK now offers their service to the public during nonprime time at a fraction of the cost professional clients pay. You can get reports, articles, magazines, journals, and government studies on countless subjects. Abstracts are also provided, and you can "download" them directly to your own computer. BRS AFTER DARK is a storehouse of material for research.

Others described in *The Phone Book* are: DELPHI, Dow Jones, CompuServe, Electronic Information Exchange System, KNOWLEDGE INDEX, NewsNet, and THE SOURCE. I'm sure this list doesn't begin to exhaust the possibilities. New sources are being offered each month. But perhaps this is enough to whet your appetite and to convince you that computers can help you with research information for sermons.

But that's not all they can do to help you with exegesis. How do you take down notes from the commentaries as you study them? A dictation machine? Yellow pad and pencil? Underlining the sentences and making notations in the margins? (That's not a seminary library book you're marking up is it?) In my sermon preparation days, B.C. (before computers), I usually took handwritten notes on the verses as I read each commentary. A new insight here, a good illustration there, and in between a clearer translation. I took them down laboriously on a legal pad. Even with my ingenious system of biblical and theological shorthand, it was slow and tedious.

Then, since my notes were grouped under each commentary as I studied it, I had to cut and paste my memos in order to compile them into a single exegesis. I also used what I thought was a clever method of transferring salient ideas and illustrations into folders, each one holding material on one point or division of the sermon. Good opening story? Drop it in the "Introduction" folder. Concise application of verse 6? That belongs in the folder for the third point of the message. Great illustration, but it doesn't seem to fit anywhere? Hold it in the "Misc." folder. Later, I can work it in whether it fits or not; it's too good to hold until next Sunday!

At last, with all the research completed and neatly categorized, it was time to polish the outline, and start putting the meat on the bones. With some variations, this familiar pattern was my style. The basic elements of it are still in place, but the computer has upgraded my style and reduced the "busy-work."

Simultaneously, while writing this book, I'm also working on the sermon I'm to preach at the Southern Baptist Convention in Kansas City. Right now, I'm plowing through a dozen commentaries on the Scripture passages the Lord has impressed me to use. As I come across a thought I want to take down, I pause for a moment in memory of my retired legal pads, and quickly write it out on the keyboard of the Model 4P.

At this stage, I'm more concerned about speed than accuracy, so I cut loose with my fastest rate of typing. (A little slower than my printer's 200 words a minute.) The order in which I take down the notes is not important either. I can move them where I want them later. Since it's easy to do on the computer, I also type in a key word with each reference to indicate the point of the sermon it seems to address. Or, if I'm not sure where it fits, I just give it a generic label such as "illustration," for example. Later, the word processor's search feature lets me pull together all those notes that belong in a certain category, and my sermon research file is quickly assimilated. Besides, I can save the notes on a disk for later reference should I preach on this text again. The sheer ease with which additions and changes are made will impress you. You'll never go back to the old ways.

Outlining and Writing the Sermon

With basic research and exegesis completed, the next step in preparing a sermon is to compose its content. Most preaching books suggest that you begin by developing a sermon thesis, that is, a concise statement of what you want to say. You probably had one in mind when you chose a text or began plowing through the commentaries, but now's the time to put the finishing touches on a clear statement of purpose. Otherwise, your message may not possess that essential quality of unity.

If the congregation is to comprehend it, your sermon must have clarity and coherence. Listeners don't like to struggle as they unravel the development of your thesis. So give them a clear outline to help them. Even if you don't intend to enumerate the usual "three points," your sermon should still have an outline. If the preacher doesn't organize his sermon, if he fails to unify his ideas and order its parts, he can't expect his listeners to search for the unity or uncover the structure in order to understand it.

In his classic, *How to Read a Book,* Mortimer J. Adler suggested that reading and writing are reciprocal arts. A logical outline is important to both writer and reader (or preacher and listener). The preacher starts with the skeleton and tries to *cover it up.* The listener tries to *uncover* the skeleton which the sermon conceals. Although he was primarily aiming at book writers, Adler's advice is applicable to sermon writers, too.

> His aim is to conceal the skeleton artistically, or, in other words, to put flesh on the bare bones. If he is a good writer, he does not bury a puny skeleton under a mass of fat; on the other hand, neither should the flesh be too thin, so that the bones show through. If the flesh is thick enough, and if flabbiness is avoided, the joints will be detected and the motion of the parts will reveal the articulation.[2]

So, with a clear thesis before him to preserve the sermon's unity, and a logical outline to preserve its coherence, the preacher is ready to "put the meat on the bones."

Do you write out your sermons in manuscript form? Homiletics experts may differ on many elements of sermon preparation, but on one point they're almost unanimous. Namely, that preparing a full manuscript can transform mediocre sermons into better sermons. Sure, there are weeks when your time gets eaten up by those unplanned events which circle your schedule like hungry vultures. In spite of noble intentions to the contrary, even homiletical purists have to settle, at times, for a hurried, sketchy outline in place of a carefully prepared manuscript.

I remember many a frantic Saturday night, when haunted by a ticking clock, I rushed through the final steps of preparation, reluctantly concluding that an "expanded" outline was all I had time to prepare. But, at the same time, I must admit that my better sermons were those I carefully wrote word for word, revised, corrected, improved, and maybe even totally rewrote. Although I never memorized my manuscripts, preparing one helped me master my material better. Besides, whenever I put down precisely what I wanted to say, I entered the pulpit armed not only with the spiritual confidence that comes from dependence on the Holy Spirit, but with that special confidence that comes from being prepared.

But whether you compose a full text or create a detailed outline, you have to do extensive writing, fleshing out the skeleton with the real content of the sermon. That's when a word processor gives you valuable assistance.

Electronic Writing

From the initial stages of research to the final manuscript, sermon preparation involves lots of writing. Writing is a craft, like carpentry, with its own tools: words, grammar, syntax, style. Like carpentry, writing skills can be learned. The tools can be mastered. Since writing is the logical arrangement of thought, if you're able to think clearly, you should be able to write clearly.

However, in order to sharpen his skills, the writer must be able to *see* his work so he can repeatedly revise it until it says what he intended. In spite of his best efforts at a first draft, the writer's sentences may be muddy instead of transparent; illogical instead of convincing. They become boring, pompous, or cluttered with unnecessary words. Lacking rhythm, the phrases may plod clumsily across the page. These are the flaws a conscientious writer attacks as he hones his craft. He places his composition before him and fiddles with it until it's right.

Dictating to a secretary may be convenient and quick; but, if you want to improve your writing, you must *see* your words before you. Our spoken sentences are usually full of repetition and sloppy constructions, which don't translate well to the written page. Furthermore, a secretary, typing from a dictating machine, can easily misunderstand; and, unless you read what's been typed, you may discover it's not what you meant. That can be embarrassing.

In Texas years ago, during a heated campaign against horse race gambling, I received a letter expressing concern about "pari-mutuel betting." Obviously, the letter had been dictated but never proofread. Instead of "pari-mutuel betting," the secretary had understood her boss to say, "her mutual bedding!" It sounded evil, but I couldn't be certain from the letter what moral issue we were fighting.

So, seeing is a key to writing. By seeing words instead of merely speaking them, the writer can recognize more readily where improvements need to be made. This visual advantage in composition has been greatly enhanced by word processors. They help polish our writing by displaying the words for our consideration and giving us an instant chance to reconsider them. For this reason, more and more preachers and other craftsmen with words are switching to electronic writing, watching their words appear on the screen and discovering how much easier it is to manipulate these tools of the trade. Why not you?

I had an experience a few weeks ago that may convince you to join the trend. He's one of those metropolitan church pastors who shared his sermon preparation style in the meeting I told you about earlier. We're good friends, so I knew he wouldn't mind my stopping by his study unannounced. His secretary led me through his regular office to a library/study where he was busy writing a book.

"My editor said its either finish this manuscript, or else!" he said. "So I'm squeezing in some writing every free moment I can." The scene was familiar to everyone who's ever written a sermon or anything else for that matter: large desk covered with material with not one square inch of its wooden surface exposed; a dozen books, each stacked open on top of the other; magazines with paper clips marking passages; photocopies of other material scattered about. Any writer would have felt right at home. I could've sat down in his chair and picked up the task with no trouble—except for one thing.

There it was right in front of him on the desk: a diminuitive, ancient portable typewriter. Ugh! It had a repulsive look. I didn't realize how far I had come in the short time since I adopted word processing. Even though I tried to squelch it, I'm sure a glimmer of self-righteous superiority momentarily shattered my usual composure. A condescending sense of pity welled up inside as I looked at that pathetic relic from the past—the typewriter, that is, not the preacher! It looked "Paleolithic" compared to my TRS-80.

I listened as my friend proudly described the writing process he had used for years: looking up material, tapping out notes on the aging typewriter, cutting and pasting these under various categories, and then composing it all into a first draft. That's where he was when I came in—on the first draft.

"Here's a sample sheet," he said, handing me a piece of paper, which upon examination, looked strangely familiar. It was exactly like sheets of my own writing in earlier days—double-spaced, typed edge to edge without margins, its lines all askew from failing to get the paper back in position after a correction. It was a mess. There were strikeovers, entire sections "X-ed" out, and holes worn through by a zealous eraser. Rose-colored lint left by the erasers still clung to the page. Two paragraphs had been circled by pencil, and a hand-drawn arrow pointed to another place in the text where he wanted them inserted. There were a few words scratched out and replaced with handwritten synonymns. "It's about ready to be typed one more time," he said. "And then I'll give it to the secretary to prepare a clean copy. After I proofread that, she'll correct it and send the final manuscript to that pushy editor." Having written several "best-sellers" over the years, he had gotten used to this procedure. For him, it sufficed, but turning to leave, I took one last glance at the antique typewriter, and I knew beyond any shadow of a doubt I would never go back.

For a moment there in his study I saw myself at work on writing projects before the Model 4P came into my life. When composing a sermon, or a book, I had differed from him in only one regard. I never could compose directly on the typewriter. When the collected notes and quotes were to be collated into a first draft, I always wrote it out by hand, relying on my legal pads and a "bouquet" of sharpened pencils—you know, a handful of golden, freshly sharpened Number Twos, dropped, eraser first, into a container so that the uniform lead points fan out into a bouquet of cedar and graphite. That distinctive aroma given off by freshly sharpened pencils still stirs in me an urge to write.

Admittedly, arranging a new box of pencils had often consumed an undue amount of time, especially during that painful period when you can't get started, when you busy yourself with getting everything ready. Many a great sermon waited to be written until each pencil was run through the electric sharpener one more time and gathered with others to be dropped jauntily into a vase. Now rub your hands together. Be sure you have enough legal pads handy. Reshuffle your material and stack it next to the pencils. Rearrange the pencils one more time. Now you're ready to write. Oops! The time is gone; you'll have to start all over again tomorrow. That was the way I used to do it.

My writing style was slow and tedious. Even with sharpened pencils and my special shorthand, it was slow. When the creative juices were really flowing, my fingers could never keep pace with my thoughts. Whoever said, "let your fingers do the walking," never tried to keep up with the brain in putting ideas on paper with a pencil. Your fingers have to run, not walk. And hurrying only makes it worse. My manuscripts were sometimes as unreadable as a doctor's prescription. Believe me, it's embarrassing to take your sermon notes to a pharmacist and ask him to decipher what you've written!

Now, all that has changed. The keyboard of the model 4P doesn't intimidate me like the old typewriter did. Oh, at first I had some trouble getting used to it. Sometimes I would get ahead of my fingers on the keys, putting spaces within words, or hitting keys too many times. Somme of m y se nt e nces look ed some ething lik e th is, and I spent a lot of time backing up the cursor to make corrections. In fact, the "left cursor" key became my favorite; the little finger on my right hand became so familiar with its location I could strike it without even lookingg. Oops! There I go again.

But don't worry about errors; they're so easily corrected, you feel free to type at maximum speed. What's more, your manual dexterity improves the more you practice. After awhile, you begin to type fast enough to keep up with your thoughts, getting those precious flashes of insight on the screen before they fade. It's easy to come back and delete, reword, or correct what's wrong. (Wouldn't it be great if *all* human error were that easy to correct?)

Furthermore, with the computer, you can work on several projects at once. For example, when I think of something I'd like to add to my Convention sermon notes, I "close the document" on this chapter I'm writing, and replace it with the "Convention Sermon" disk. I "open" the new document and call for a "search string," which is the computer's way of helping you go quickly to any location in your composition by searching for a certain word or "string" of letters. Insert the word you want it to find, and, buzz, whir, hum. A message appears: "One Moment Please," and there it is. The cursor is blinking at the very spot you want to revise. It always works, except when a misspelled word in your search string sends the disk drive on a wild-goose chase. Machines have no feelings, I know, but mine seems to express disappointment when it ends a futile search with the message: "Can't find ****"

No, I would never go back. It now seems perfectly natural

to compose material directly on the keys of the word processor, eliminating most of the tedious steps of the old-fashioned style. Revisions are easy, and you can either choose to keep the old edition for later reference or save the new one, or both. When you're through, you're ready to print a perfect copy in whatever format you choose. I hope someday I can convince my slow-writing friend that it's the only way to go. He could be so much more productive if he retired his ancient typewriter and joined the revolutionary new world of computers. And so could you.

Potential Pitfalls

There are pitfalls in computer writing. The machine has what one author called "a dark underbelly." Things can go wrong. Words printed on paper have a comforting, visible permanence to them. You know without a doubt they exist. Words on paper can be safely folded up in a manila folder, fastened on a clipboard, or snapped into a three-ring binder. They exist. I'm not so sure about words on a screen. Scientists say computer words are nothing more than pixels of light projected on the screen by a cathode ray tube. They don't seem to exist in the real sense I have always thought written words existed.

At the beginning of my pilgrimage into computer writing, I had some serious doubts. Couldn't something happen accidentally—the wrong key pushed, a power failure, or an attack by one of those demonic gremlins that plague any electronic device I put my hands on? Couldn't these words that semiexist on the screen just vanish into thin air? (There's no air any thinner than the air into which a preacher starting out on a computer fears his words will vanish.) Or, just as frightening, if I followed the manual and stored my freshly-written sermon overnight on a disk, would I be able to call it back in the morning? The chances of ever seeing any sermon stored on something called "floppy" struck me as exceedingly low.

But that was beginner's fear. Now after several years of

experience, I *know* things can go wrong! Let me illustrate. I remember well the first time I tried to show off my new computer skills to my family. With wife, sister, brothers, and assorted in-laws gathered around my desk, I suggested confidently that my microcomputer could simplify a tedious but necessary task. It was following my father's funeral. There were stacks of cards and paper notes with names of people who had brought food, sent flowers, or mailed personal greetings. The family wanted to respond to each of these, making certain no one was overlooked. I boldly claimed that my computer and I had the solution.

I organized the family and then sat down at the console of my computer. While one person called out the names, another looked up the addresses, and I typed the information under certain categories: food, flowers, memorial gifts, or greetings. After an hour of hard work, punctuated by familial compliments on my computer ability, the impossible happened. I'd been sitting for a long time, so I shifted my chair, and moved the computer to a new position in front of me. The power strip into which I had plugged all my equipment was beside the computer. As I changed positions, my hand bumped against the power strip switch and turned it off. The screen went blank.

I recall saying something like, "Oops! I accidentally flipped a switch, just a second while I get it back on." Now, up until then, the "foreverness" of a switched-off computer was something I had never experienced firsthand. But when the screen came back on again with its usual start-up messages, I knew. I fiddled with disks and key strokes, but deep down inside, I knew. Everything was lost! *And I think they knew, too.* Even though I came up with something like: "Let's start all over, I believe there's a better way to organize this"; they knew. It was humbling to say the least; but it taught me that things can go wrong.

You don't have to accidentally touch a switch. A bolt of lightning can do it. Static electricity can do it. Not paying your electric bill can do it. When the computer goes off, whatever you've written disappears forever. You stare into space wondering where in the invisible world of electricity your lost masterpiece now resides. You have to start over, and with luck, a few of your lost sentences come limping back; but they're seldom as scintillating as your creative originals. You've just experienced an electronic catastrophe.

Can you imagine the panic of a pastor on Saturday night at 11:30? He's at his computer, almost finished with the sermon he'll preach in the morning. He walks across the wool carpet to get a book, comes back, and zap! A static spark jumps from his finger to the computer and wipes out the entire sermon! (Satan has a new tool to use against the preacher.)

But there are precautions you can take to avoid such disasters. Every once in a while, stop, push two buttons, and wait a second while the work you've done up to that point is stored safely on its disk. It only takes a second, and it ensures that you will still have your work even if the power goes off. (In fact, I think I'll push those two buttons right now just in case!)

Don't take chances. Put a static pad under your computer. Keep the humidity high. Use a power surge plug. Above all, save your material as you go and make "backups" of your work on another disk. This is a quick and simple operation which in seconds automatically copies everything on one disk to another for safekeeping. Since it's easy, make printed copies periodically.

These computer horror stories are enough to make you fold up the book and go back to pencil and paper, but don't panic. Such losses don't occur often. It only happened to me once, before I learned to avoid disasters by taking precautions. Still, I wanted to include this section to show there is a "dark underbelly" to this otherwise beautiful beast of electronic writing. It's not all peaches and cream, but it's a remarkable new tool God has providentially provided for the proclaimer of the unchanging gospel.

Filing Sermon Material

When I was a student in the seminary, an enterprising salesman introduced us to a complex, efficient filing system. It was costly, but he convinced a lot of us we couldn't do without it in our ministry. Every clipping, illustration, book, poem, or sermon could be placed under one of the subjects in the system, cross-indexed, and readily pulled out again when you needed it. It was a good idea, but after a few months I realized that to use it properly, I would have to devote my full time to filing. Somehow, I just didn't feel called to the full-time ministry of manila folders. I returned the beautiful system to its original box, and gave it away. I suppose to this day, my slightly used box of filing materials continues to be passed on by one disappointed pastor to another. Later, I developed a simpler filing system which I've used over the years. (I also admit to an occasional use of the "second-drawer-on-the-left" method. Anything of interest is stacked in that drawer, and reviewed for relevent material each time I prepare a sermon.)

First, in my search for a simpler way, I established a sermon file. I gave each sermon a consecutive number, and filed it in its folder behind the last sermon I had preached. Over the years the file boxes full of consecutively numbered sermons have accumulated from sermon #1 to #2025. In my copy of *A Pastor's Five-Year Record Book,* I listed the number, subject, and text of each sermon as well as where I preached it.

On separate file cards, I cross-referenced the Scripture texts and subjects, so that, if I wanted to see the sermons I'd preached on "Grace," I pulled out that card, and there sermons #245, #855, and a dozen others were listed. The same is true of the Scripture file.

Since filing is one of the tasks a computer does best, I'm now transferring these paper files to the PFS:FILE system on my computer. (Remember the filing programs I described in chapter 2?) When complete, it will give me instant access to every sermon by title, subject, or text as well as separate listings of poems and illustrations. I only wish I could have started out this way thirty years ago. Not only does the computer offer advantages in filing sermons and illustrations, but you can save your study notes as well. The commentary study material and the final sermon manuscripts you store on floppy disks become a permanent file, too.

Each disk holds 174,000 characters. With the "compressed document" feature on my word processor, that's enough space to store about seventy-five pages of double-spaced, typed material, 8 1/2 by 11 inches. Most of my sermon manuscripts are about fifteen pages long, which means I can store five sermon manuscripts on one paper-thin disk. Use both sides of a floppy and you double that capacity. Add a hard disk drive to your computer and one disk can hold five million characters. In place of the twenty filing boxes of sermons stacked in three cabinets behind my desk, I could store a lifetime of sermon manuscripts in a few disks on one shelf!

Electronic filing takes less time than the paper method, and it's so much better. I'm convinced it's worth the trouble to change from your present system, even if you're at mid-career. But if you're just beginning your ministry, the reasons to start now are overwhelming.

Preaching the Sermon Again

Maybe not all of them are, but some of your sermons are worth preaching again. After a few years at a church, most of us have recycled a few of our "sugar sticks" before the same congregation. Update them, change a few stories, and if they were blessed by God the first time you preached them, try them again—unless you have a deacon in your church like I had in Houston. He opened his Bible to the text of every sermon, and marked the subject and the date in the margin. Even after several years, if I preached that sermon again, Dan would smile at me from his favorite pew, raise his hand and give me an "A-OK" signal to let me know he remembered.

I could never preach a sermon twice without his knowing it. He assured me, however, that he didn't mind hearing them again.

You may not preach your sermons again to the same congregation, but when invitations come to preach in a revival or in seminary chapel, for example, or if you move to another church field, your sermon file becomes a valuable resource. On those occasions, you'll be glad you took time to build a good filing system.

Visualize the following scenario. You have a computerized sermon filing system in place, and you've been invited by a preacher friend to speak at his building dedication service. That sermon you prepared for your own church's dedication service two years ago would be perfect for this new occasion. If you saved it on disk, you're in luck. Call up the subject: "Building Dedication" on your computer filing system to find the number of the message and the disk on which you stored it. Load the disk, and call it up on the screen.

Obviously, you'll need to make some changes in the sermon. After all, in Houston, you wouldn't want to say, "We are here in Fort Worth today to dedicate this beautiful building." But changes are no trouble. Read through the manuscript on the screen, making whatever revisions you like, and then print out a perfect edition for the building dedication service. You can print on regular 8 1/2 x 11" paper; double, triple, or any space; use a variety of type styles; or print on smaller notebook paper or cards—whatever your customary method calls for. When the printing is completed, your original is still there on the disk, along with your revised, updated version, waiting for the next invitation to preach a dedication sermon. After you preach at the other church, throw that manuscript away. There's no need to clutter up your study with unnecessary paper files.

If only this amazing system had been available years ago. I've preached some of my favorite sermons in dozens of locations, and my manuscripts show it. When you've erased the names of twelve different towns in order to write in another, your notes begin to disintegrate. Even with few changes, sermon notes used dozens of times begin to look like they've been used dozens of times. Wouldn't it be great to take an old favorite into the pulpit looking like it just came out of the typewriter? As a matter of fact it just did, if you have a computer.

Maybe I get carried away in my enthusiasm for computer-assisted preaching, but I believe my enthusiasm is well-founded. The possibilities for computer applications in sermon preparation are already abundant, and new ones are appearing every day. In this chapter, I've only touched the hem of a huge, growing garment. The best is yet to be.

I could have added another chapter on using the computer for writing articles, curriculum materials, newsletters, and books. The word processor is just as effective for these purposes too. I only hope that whatever your writing task may be, you've been encouraged to employ this new electronic technology. Who knows, someday you might be asked to write a book on "Computers and the Minister."

Notes

1. Mike Cane, *The Computer Phone Book,* New American Library (New York: Times Mirror, 1983).
2. Mortimer J. Adler, *How to Read a Book* (New York: Simon and Schuster, 1940), pp. 90-91.

4
The Personal Computer and Visitation and Evangelism

"Reaching people" is a popular term used today for those church activities which are designed to lead people to faith in Christ and membership in the church. I don't know when or where the term was first given this special meaning, but looking up the dictionary definition of the verb "to reach," I can understand why it was used. To reach means to extend, to stretch, to thrust out, to penetrate to, to arrive at, to have influence on, or to get in touch with, to contact. Each one of these action words can be appropriately applied to the church's evangelistic effort to share Christ with the lost. Because it emphasizes the initiative, the intensity, the effort, and the enthusiasm we should have when we witness, to reach are accurate words to use.

To me, it always sounded grammatically incorrect to say, "He reached me an orange," but Webster says it's OK. I discovered, to my surprise, that the fourth of several definitions of to reach is "to obtain and deliver to someone else." In fact, that very sentence, which sounds so awkward, is the one the dictionary used as a correct example: "He reached me an orange." So, unlikely as it may sound, it's another acceptable synonym for evangelism. We reach people the gospel. We reach them hope and forgiveness. We reach them new life, and the joy of fellowship with Christ. When we witness, we're not only reaching lost persons, we're "obtaining and delivering" to them the opportunity to receive by faith God's unspeakable gift of salvation. Sounds exciting, doesn't it?

Specifically, reaching people means making direct personal visits or telephone calls to prospects, but a broader definition includes numerous other activities which indirectly encourage the unchurched to respond. Recreation, craft classes, weekday schools, medical clinics, when offered to nonmembers, are, by this broader definition, legitimate "outreach programs." But it's the narrower definition of reaching people that concerns us here—that is, directly contacting those who need to accept Christ as Savior or who need to join a local congregation.

Sometimes that direct contact is most effective when it comes about because of an unexpected experience. Remember that time you didn't deliberately set out to witness, but God interrupted your schedule with the surprise appearance of someone who needed to hear about Christ? This is "oblique" witnessing, "serendipitous" outreach. An unforeseen turn in a conversation, an unexpected phone call, a chance encounter—these occasions become never-to-be-repeated opportunities to witness. How easy they are to overlook if we're not alert to recognize them when they come.

He called for an appointment to talk about a term theme he was writing at Georgia Tech, and I was flattered. A brilliant chemistry student, he wanted me to help him understand some of the philosophical distinctions he had encountered in his study of comparative religions. Since I had majored in philosophy of religion at the seminary, and his topic was right down my alley, I was ready for him when he came for the appointment.

After what I humbly believed was a scintillating intellectual response on my part, for which I was humbly sure he would be eternally grateful, he stood to leave. He thanked me. And then, hesitating, he said, almost reluctantly, "One of these days, pastor, I need to talk to you about my own personal relationship with God." Caught up in admiration for my great intellectual performance, I heard myself answering, "Good, call my secretary and make another appointment, and we'll talk."

Then it dawned on me. He hadn't really come to talk about the research paper at all. He had come to talk about his own spiritual life, and I had nearly missed the opportunity. I had been so preoccupied with the exhilarating intellectualism of our discussion that my spiritual sensitivity was nearly inoperative. Thankfully, I stopped myself in mid-sentence, and said, "Why don't we do that right now." We sat back down. He acknowledged he was not a believer. We read the Bible and prayed together, and he asked Jesus to save him. Later, after I had the privilege of baptizing him, he graduated from Georgia Tech and moved to another state where he's active in a small Baptist church. When I hear from him, as I still do occasionally, it reminds me how close I came to overlooking one of those rare, spontaneous opportunities to witness.

Paul's command in Colossians to redeem the time, sometimes translated, "make the most of the time," calls us to be spiritually sensitive to unplanned opportunities like that. So as ministers, not only are we to be alert, but we are to train our people to be perpetually alert to unpredictable "close encounters" which God regularly drops in our pathway as occasions for witness.

Reaching people also includes "life-style" or "cultivation" evangelism. If you make friends with non-Christians, live before them an exemplary Christian life-style, and nurture the relationship until they trust you, eventually they will ask about your faith. You will have earned the opportunity to tell them. It's a long-range approach, but a very effective outreach strategy.

But unplanned witnessing and life-style evangelism in no way diminish the importance of deliberate, intentional witnessing through the outreach ministry of the church. Those Thursday nights when you meet for church visitation, take a prospect card, drive to that unfamiliar street, knock on the door, and talk to a stranger about his or her relationship with God—that's basic. That's the church's bread-and-butter strategy to get outreach done. And it's that deliberate, specific strategy of evangelistic visitation I believe computer technology can help us improve.

The Importance of Evangelistic Records

To know by name, age, and location the persons in the community who need to be contacted is an absolute necessity in implementing church growth principles. One characteristic, common to all growing churches, is that they all maintain an up-to-date prospect file. Some churches use door-to-door religious censuses, others divide telephone book pages among their members and survey sections of the community by telephone. New move-in lists secured from utility companies, collection agencies, and welcome groups are used by some congregations to keep their files current.

One church formed a consortium with five other churches in the neighborhood to employ a visitor to secure religious census information from new residents. Larger congregations sometimes have their own staff to maintain the file. However it is assembled, there must be a prospect file if the church is to reach people.

Prospects are everywhere, and with a little imagination you can devise creative methods of discovering them. Since research indicates most church members can name eight unchurched or unsaved people among their friends and relatives, start there. Survey your membership. That should provide you with a prospect file nearly eight times the size of your church roll. Add to that the names of the nonmembers who send their children to your Vacation Bible School, youth camps, or day schools. Then, there are the visitors who show up for music or dramatic presentations, and others who attend Easter, Christmas, and Mother's Day. A church in Fort Worth sends out teams who have worshipped at 8:30 AM to visit people who are in their yards during the 11:00 AM worship service. They're obviously not churchgoers, and many are prospects.

Even though it's overused by the advertising world, mass

mailing is an effective device for discovering prospects. We tried it effectively in Atlanta. Identifying a section of the city by zip codes, we secured mass mailing lists, and sent each resident in that section an invitation to attend a "Pastor's Bible Study Class" meeting in the church auditorium. We slanted the invitation toward non-Sunday School types who knew very little about the Bible and might feel uncomfortable in a regular class. Discussion in the class, which ran for only six Sunday mornings, addressed some of the contemporary questions people were asking: "Is There Life After Death?" "Is the World Coming to an End?" "Are Demons and Angels Real?" "What About Miracles?" "Is Jesus the Only Way to God?" "Who are Southern Baptists?" At the end of the series, we would encourage those who attended to join a regular Sunday School class, and, of course, we placed them on our prospect file for continuing follow-up. Then, after a brief interlude, we sent invitations to another section of the city and started all over again.

Knowing the importance of maintaining an active, up-to-date prospect file, if I were the minister responsible, I would employ the personal computer to help me. The programs described in the preceding chapter would make it easy to store, update, organize, and print lists of prospects by various categories. Match them with church or Sunday School members with similar characteristics and you have the basics of a very effective visitation program. If you're the pastor of a smaller church who must single-handedly maintain the prospect file and distribute visitation assignments, the personal computer can help immensely.

For example, with a simple filing program like the PFS:FILE software I use with my TRS-80 model 4P, you can design your own basic prospect form for each family or individual. When you're satisfied with the information you wish to list, all you do is fill in the blanks. You can enter the data in any order you like, save it, and find it quickly when you need it. Updating, correcting, or changing the form is easy.

You can then retrieve the information in a variety of ways. Ask the computer to find all the prospects who live in zip code area 76115, or in zone 4, an area which you have defined. Ask it to give you all the prospects over fifty years of age, or all who are over fifty, who live in zone 4, who have college age children, and who are not members of any church. Depending on the facts you decided to include in your prospect form, you can call for any combination you want. You can see the possibilities.

PFS:FILE is not only one of the easiest programs to use, it's also an easy one to learn. Unlike so many others, the manual was written by a writer, not a computer technician, so it's readable, using language even we uninitiated can understand. Furthermore, there's a helpful glossary of terms and an appendix that interprets error messages and unravels those pesky complications we amateurs often get into. PFS:FILE, a relatively inexpensive program with editions for most popular personal computers, can handle not only a prospect file effectively, but, as we'll see in a later chapter, it can manage other ministerial records as well.

The Minister's Personal Prospect File

This chapter has a slightly different focus. What we want to explore here is how a pastor or ministerial staff member can use a computer in his own *personal* program of evangelistic visitation.

I believe a minister ought to have his own prospect list, taken from the general file, to which he gives his personal attention. It would consist of families and individuals who, for some reason, need special attention. They may have requested a ministerial call, or be someone with whom the minister has a unique relationship. Whatever the reason, they're your special group to pray for and visit. The computer's power to manipulate information about them enables you to keep up with a greater number of them with greater detail. Since the filing program is so easy to use, this is one list I suggest you maintain yourself. Secretaries or other staff members can relieve you of the responsibility of the official church prospect file, but maintaining your own visitation list on the computer is more efficient. To begin with, the computer is immediately accessible, on your office desk, or at home. You can skip the "middle man" and the delay inherent in reporting and receiving information through others. Each time you make a visit, you pick up additional details about the prospect which, with very little effort, you can add to the other facts in your file. As their personal profile grows, so does your understanding of the person's needs. A review of this enlarging resume before the next visit can make your witness all the more effective.

Let the computer remind you each day of significant events in the prospect's life—a birthday, an anniversary, the beginning of a new job, upcoming surgery, a high school senior's graduation, or the day a family's first child leaves for college. These are occasions when your personal witness by phone, note, or visit can be used by the Holy Spirit to the greatest advantage.

Granted, nothing can substitute for a face-to-face visit, but the telephone is almost as effective. In a tight situation, when a personal visit is impossible, wouldn't the following imaginary situation work for you? You have your personal prospect list on the computer in your study at home. It's Saturday afternoon, and you've just come in from your weekly battle with a runaway lawn. You've let the time get away, and now, because you have a wedding in two hours, there's no time to make the visits you had planned to make. But you have an alternative. Sit down at your keyboard with a sparkling glass of iced tea and pull up the file on the Jack Hollis family who ought to join the church tomorrow. The phone number is there on the screen and so is Jack's wife's name and the names of his teenage daughter and son.

(In making a phone call, few things are more embarrassing

than suddenly realizing, after two rings, that you don't remember Jack Hollis's wife's first name. "Namenesia" can set in at the most inappropriate times! Frantically, as you hear the third ring, you yell to your wife in the den, "Honey! What's Jack Hollis's wife's first name?" You're too late! A feminine voice on the other end of the line answers just in time to hear the bellowing reverberations of your last three words. Now, you have to think of something quick. What will you call her? "Mrs. Hollis" sounds too formal. "Hello Dearie" too familiar. In a fumbling attempt to smooth things over, you shift into your cheeriest voice and say, "Well, hello there, is your husband home?" Good try, but not good enough. The problem is that you're speaking not to Mrs. Hollis, but to her daughter. "Oh, sorry, I though you were, uh . . . (What *is* that woman's name!) . . . that is, your mother." You've blown it. Or as the teenagers say, "That was uncool.")

Since the information is right there on the screen, you're ready with a name, no matter who answers the phone. You even see that Jason, their son, plays quarterback on the high school football team, so if he answers, you can ask about the team. The screen reminds you when you were last in their home, what their excuses were, what Sunday School class they would be in, and that Jack's mother in Dallas has been very ill.

Imagine how much more effective you'll be, armed with such detailed information, as you encourage their church membership decision, pray over the phone for Jack's mother in Dallas, and tell them you'll see them in church tomorrow. All the while, if you've learned to cradle a telephone between your ear and your shoulder, you can be typing in the new information you've discovered about Jack and Jill Hollis. (Sure, you remembered her name.) When you hang up, all the data is there in the computer ready for your next contact, or better, to help you introduce the Hollis family when they join tomorrow. In the time it would take you to drive to one family, you can have a quality visit with several, finish your glass of iced tea, and still have time to dress for the wedding.

Using the computer in this way doesn't mean your contact is impersonal or mechanical. It doesn't cheapen your witness. On the contrary, by giving you a greater capacity to monitor details, the computer reinforces the personal nature of your visit, and actually enhances the quality of your witness.

Pastoral Calling

The same kind of computerized monitoring of visitation applies to pastoral calling as well. In addition to evangelistic visiting, the minister also regularly calls on church members. It's a unique privilege given to the minister. No other profession has an open door to call at any time. The physician, the lawyer, and the teacher have to wait for invitations in order to be ethical. But by the very nature of his vocation, the minister doesn't have to wait for his members to invite him. He has the unique professional privilege to visit in the homes of the congregation at any time.

Dr. George Buttrick said that if he did not make at least 1,000 calls a year, he could not preach intelligently to his congregation's needs. Bishop Gerald Kennedy made this confession:

> As a young minister I could not believe that punching doorbells and stopping by to see folks was worthy of my educational accomplishments. This seemed such a useless waste of my time and energy. . . . Today, however, I know of its importance. I would be a better pastor if I had it to do over again.[1]

There are three major types of pastoral calls, according to C. W. Brister: (1) routine calls, in which the church's message and fellowship are carried regularly to some persons and families; (2) crucial calling, in which Christian resources are offered to those experiencing crises or distress; and (3) casual contacts, in which the minister encounters persons in unstructured settings, yet seeks to make such contacts vital. The calls may be made by telephone, visits in homes, hospitals, businesses, or wherever the minister encounters his people.[2]

Even though some pastoral visitation can be categorized as "casual" or "routine," the need for readily available and accurate information about the persons being visited is essential. Here again is where the personal computer can help you. An up-to-date file on computer disks of the families and individuals in the membership is a valuable tool. Keeping records of visits made to these people, even though it takes time, is of great value to the minister too. Chapter 7 on record keeping illustrates how the personal computer can be helpful in this area.

A Computer in Your Car

While we're exploring new ways to improve your visitation procedures, let me run another idea by you. I've always had a weakness for gadgets, especially electronic gadgets. It was during my pastorate in Houston that those telephone "beepers" first became so popular, especially among the medical profession. Unlike the latest beepers which not only signal you from your office, but also relay brief audible or visible messages, these early models did nothing more than beep when someone called your number. You then had to find a phone and return the call to your office to receive your message. The telephone company had an introductory offer to try one of theirs for a month, so I did. It really didn't prove to be very helpful, but I had a lot of fun with it before returning it.

After pastors conference one Monday, a group of us were having lunch in a cafeteria. In our luncheon group was one of those characters who always knows the latest news. You could never tell him anything he hadn't already heard. There was never a new development he was not aware of, no gadget he hadn't already examined or put to use. Mention some revolutionary new discovery that had just been announced, and he would douse cold water on your enthusiasm by saying,

"You mean you're just now hearing about that? I've known about it for months."

Knowing he would be at the table with us about 12:30, I arranged for my secretary to call my borrowed beeper's number at that time. When it buzzed, catching everybody's attention, I casually pulled it out of my coat pocket, turned it off, and then put it to my mouth as if it were a two-way radio. "Yes, what is it?" I said quietly. Then I put it to my ear as if to hear a message from my office. For a few minutes, I carried on an imaginary conversation, switching the beeper from mouth to ear, and even writing down a phone number and name that supposedly came over my amazing portable telephone. Finally, I said good-bye, and casually replaced the machine in my pocket.

Everyone was aghast! They all began to exclaim over the gadget and wanted to see it and try it out—everyone but you-know-who. He tried to appear uninterested and unimpressed, and mumbled something like, "Oh yeah. I know all about those. They've been out for awhile." For a wonderful few minutes, before I explained my joke, we all enjoyed watching our friend struggle to act unimpressed and maintain his cool composure in the midst of excitement. When I admitted it was all a joke, our smug Mr. "Know-it-all" defended his honor by adding, "Well, of course I knew you couldn't *talk* on those things."

Well, what was incredible then is rather ordinary now. The electronic beeper does more than beep. It relays messages. And we're not far from the time when a remote telephone can be carried in a pocket. Wouldn't it be wonderful if your car could be equipped as a portable ministerial office? All those unproductive hours when you're on the way to something else or stuck on a crowded freeway could be redeemed. Such a dream may be closer than we think. Cellular telephone systems are being installed in major cities now, prices are coming down, and it won't be long before car telephones will be practical for most ministers. We already have sophisticated portable dictating equipment which can be used while driving, and now there are portable computers you can operate in your automobile. While we're stretching our imaginations, let me try out another scenario on you.

I have a TRS-80 model 100 briefcase computer which I described in detail earlier. Powered by four AA penlight batteries, which in turn keep a cadmium battery charged to hold the memory while turned off, the Model 100 operates about twenty hours without an AC power source. If you have the 32K model, as I do, you can store about twenty pages of text in the computer. That's enough capacity to perform most of the personal visitation tasks I described, but with the added convenience of portability. Do you mean I can operate a computerized personal visitation file in my car? That's right. Here's how it works.

The Model 100 comes with five built-in programs which you can learn in a very short time. I mentioned earlier that the instruction manuals for this computer are clear and easy to understand. Both the computer and its manuals are User-friendly with a capital U. The address file program can be used to record the same basic data on your personal prospects as the PFS:FILE program keeps on your desk top computer. (As a matter of fact, since the Model 100 can be used on a desk as well as in the car, you could get by on it very well for both applications.)

There is a simple search function by which you can call up a name from the file even if all you remember is that the person lives somewhere on Maple Avenue. Switch on your computer. The screen displays a list of your programs. (Yes, the Model 100 has a screen like a desktop computer, only smaller.) Move the cursor to the address program. Push the "enter" key to load it. Push the "find" key, and type in Maple Avenue. In a flash, there on your screen, are the names of all those prospects who live on Maple Avenue, including the Gordons, the family you were trying to find. The basic information about the Gordons is there, but you might want more detailed notes than that. So go back to the text preparation (word processing) program and punch up your notes on the Gordons. All the personal data you've been gathering on this family is there ready for your review.

Now, you're back behind the wheel after visiting the Gordon family. A block or two away you pull to the curb, call up their file again, and type in the additional information you've learned about them along with the date of your visit. Switch to the address file again, find another prospect who lives in the same zip code area, and while you're on the way to their house, review the detailed personal information about them on the screen so you'll be prepared.

A word of warning, though. Driving while computering (DWC) can be dangerous to your health and to the safety of others. And, besides that, some traffic patrolmen may not yet be as enthusiastic about the new world of computerized visitation as you are. "Well you see, officer, I ran that red light because I was scrolling through my prospects with my cursor control button." Hollow laughter while offering such an excuse to an unsmiling police officer has seldom been known to discourage a traffic citation.

But used with common sense and good judgment, the portable computer in the car can be quite an advantage to a minister on the go, or to anyone on the go for that matter. In the *Dallas Morning News* recently there was a picture of taxi driver Chris Gomez, his left hand on the wheel of his cab, and his right hand manipulating the keys of a TRS-80 Model 100. Mounted ingeniously on the dash within easy reach, his portable is programmed to help Gomez find streets more quickly.

It's a great idea. By transferring the street index of the city map into the computer, along with some simple directions, the driver can instantly find the location to which his fare wants to go. Furthermore, he has entered the addresses and phone numbers of the major hotels and restaurants in town. When a customer asks for a place by name, he types it in on the keyboard and gets an address or map reference number.

"My tips alone have almost tripled since I've had the computer in the car," Gomez said. "Now it's a conversation piece. I show the customers all kinds of things I've done with it. It's a new concept that's really going to take off." Adopt a similar technique, and while your tips may not, your efficiency will at least triple as you make your ministerial visits.

The popularity of the briefcase or notebook computer is growing. Physicians and surgeons are using it as they make their hospital rounds. Traveling salespersons, reporters, engineers, executives who do business in several cities, real estate agents, coaches—all of whom need information readily at hand wherever they are—have picked up on the advantages of this powerful, four-pound marvel. If a cabby and a computer can pair up to save time and money, why can't a minister and a machine pair up to make personal visitation time more productive?

There are other capabilities of the briefcase computer which are beyond the scope of this book to describe, but mentioning a few may encourage you to investigate further. When you plug it into a telephone receptacle, for example, it becomes an automatic dialer. Type in a name, punch the "call" button, and it dials the number automatically. You can even include the code numbers of your money-saving long distance service to make out-of-town calls. The Model 100 can access information services, plug into electronic libraries, send electronic mail, and can exchange information with your desktop unit. If you exceed the memory capacity of the Model 100, you can save information on a cassette tape for future reference. And because it does a fairly good job of word processing, you can write letters, reports, and other documents; connect your portable to a printer, and get a perfect copy.

As its popularity grows, there is springing up around the TRS-80 Model 100 a complex network of additional software programs, peripheral devices, a special magazine called *Portable 100,* numerous books, and several enthusiastic user groups. Perhaps some of you with a gift for electronics can discover and make available new ministry applications for the portable computer the rest of us never dreamed of. And as improvements are added, as they inevitably will be, this tiny newcomer on the scene may prove to be a minister's best computer tool.

Notes

1. Quoted in Eugene Stowe, *The Ministry of Shepherding* (Kansas City, Mo.: Beacon Hill Press, 1976), p. 100.
2. C. W. Brister, *Pastoral Care in the Church* (New York: Harper & Row, 1964), p. 150.

5
The Minister's Computer and Personal Counseling

In an effort to keep our seminary curriculum focused on the practical needs of ministry today, I've made it a practice to question our graduates when I visit their churches. I ask them, "What part of your work do you feel least prepared to do?" The answers vary, but always in the top two or three will be the task of personal counseling. Had I been asked the same question at the beginning of my ministry, it would have been at the top of my list, too. It isn't that the seminary didn't offer adequate courses in pastoral counseling, although I readily acknowledge there is always room for improvements. It's just that as a student I didn't realize how much training I would need in this area. Therefore, since counseling had very little appeal to me at the time, I chose to take only the basic required courses. Later, caught up in the unrelenting demands of an active ministry, like most of the graduates I interview, I found myself wishing I'd spent more time learning how to counsel.

Why? Because as every pastor soon learns, much, if not most, of his time each week is spent in personal counseling. Studies indicate that four in ten Americans with deep personal problems turn first to a minister for help. There are times in the pastorate when you're convinced that all 40 percent are turning to you. In my two larger pastorates, I estimate without exaggeration, that I could have spent forty hours a week just in personal counseling. As a pastor, you don't have the privilege of deciding whether or not you'll counsel; only whether or not you'll do it well. You *will* counsel. It goes with the territory. And if you feel unprepared, you'll probably do as I did. You'll learn how to be a better counselor by reading, attending seminars, or by enrolling in an academic course or a clinical program. Of course, you'll also learn by doing it, by trial and error. Experience is a good teacher, and you'll gain confidence in your own common-sense style as you practice counseling.

Whatever self-training program you adopt, you'll at least need to learn what personal counseling can accomplish, what purposes a counseling session should have, the different styles and techniques effective counselors use, how to recognize serious cases of irrational behavior that call for professional treatment, and how to refer counselees to appropriate specialists.

The fact that the pastor carries most of the counseling load for the church does not exempt other ministers on the staff from similar responsibilities. That's one reason the term "Minister" instead of "Director" is appropriate for those who serve in music, education, recreation, or other fields. You, like the pastor, will have more opportunities than you can handle to help people with their personal problems. In addition to learning the competencies needed in your specialty, you'll also need to learn how to be a counselor.

Pastoral conversation is the term C. W. Brister employed to describe both informal visits in homes and hospitals, and the more formal multiple-interview sessions we normally think of as counseling.[1] It's an accurate descriptive term because it correctly suggests that, in addition to the one-way monologues of preaching or teaching, the minister also engages regularly in two-way dialogues or conversations with individuals.

Along with evangelistic witnessing aimed at leading lost persons to faith in Jesus Christ, the minister's task also includes pastoral witnessing. When the troubled turn to you for help, you first try to win them to Christ. If they accept Him, or if they're already believers, you then have the added responsibility to help them relate the gospel to their life situation. That's pastoral witnessing.

According to Brister, there are "precounseling conversations" such as informal social contacts in the community, supportive calls in the hospital or home, instructional interviews, and brief single conversations with persons at church who ask you to pray for them. But these informal, preliminary contacts often lead to a series of more intensive, longer-termed, structured counseling conversations. Pastoral counseling, then, is "the process of conversations between a responsible minister and a concerned individual or intimate group, with the intent of enabling such persons to work through their concerns to a constructive course of action."[2]

Once you have shifted from precounseling conversations to formal counseling appointments with a person, Wayne Oates suggests that you'll normally work through five typical phases in your counseling conversation.

1. The Preparatory Phase. During this first phase, you may actually take the initiative to discover persons in need, to encourage them to ask for help, and maybe even to establish the first contact.

2. The Relaxation and Rapport Phase. Most persons with emotional problems are tense, suspicious, and self-conscious. Therefore, early in the counseling process, you must put them at ease and encourage them to trust you.

3. The Listening and Exploration Phase. This is the heart of your task as a counselor in which you help the person "talk it out" in an experience of emotional release. In order to help your counselee feel safe in expressing real feelings, you must become a skilled listener. It takes practice and deliberate effort to let the person do the talking while you try to hear accurately what the person says without appearing preoccupied or distracted. But training yourself to listen and to encourage the counselee to talk is essential to effective counseling.

4. The Reconstruction and Guidance Phase. The minister's role here is to help the person interpret the causes of his trouble, to help him define a course of action, and to refer the counselee to biblical resources, therapeutic literature, and practical goals and plans. This may be the point at which you'll wisely decide the problems you're dealing with are more serious than you can handle. They appear to point to deeper personal disorders or mental illness that call for specialized professional help. A referral is then in order.

5. The Follow-Up and Experimentation Phase. Sometimes counseling efforts go to waste because the counselor failed to follow up the progress of the persons with whom he's been counseling. The counselee is experimenting with and testing his new approach to life, and may need the reinforcement and encouragement of your continuing interest.[3]

It's clear from these definitions of counseling that although sharpening your professional techniques and therapy skills is important, it's more important to develop mutual relationships of trust and responsibility with those who come to you for help. For when a troubled person begins to trust you and express his feelings honestly, and when you become a sensitive, responsible listener who sincerely tries to understand, the healing process begins. That means that an accepting-responsive style of counseling is usually better than a rigid, manipulative, directive style. You learn to listen patiently, respond reflectively, and comment carefully so that the counselee may clarify his own feelings and assume responsibility for his own decisions.[4] The directive approach to counseling may seem more authoritative and less time-consuming, but it usually blocks the counselee's process of working through the problem. And it imposes your own personal opinions which may not be appropriate.

A cartoon I saw recently pictured an unshaven janitor with a stub of a cigar in his mouth and a mop in his hand cleaning the office of a marriage counselor. It was after hours, the psychologist had gone home, so the janitor had answered a late call from a counselee. His advice to the troubled caller is the caption under the cartoon: "Well, if it was me, I'd bust her one in the mouth!" That's the direct counseling approach, taken to an extreme!

But a nondirective counseling style can be abused as well. You don't want to be manipulative, but neither is your role as a counselor an inactive, passive one. There's a story of a minister who was proud of his nondirective style of counseling. He studiously avoided offering any advice or guidance to those who came to him for help. He listened passively and always reflected the person's feelings back to him with a question. One day, on the street corner, a stranger asked the minister, "Can you tell me how to get to the post office?" And the nondirective minister answered, "Oh, so you want to go to the post office?" That's the nondirective approach, taken to an extreme.

Effective pastoral counseling is permissive *and* persuasive, accepting *and* confronting. As a Christian minister, you not only listen acceptingly to the troubled person's feelings and help him clarify and work through them, you also have something to say. You bring a supernatural source of help to the situation by sharing the mind of Christ and the spiritual insights of revealed Christian truth. Therefore, Christian counseling goes beyond a strictly nondirective style. You can suggest unique actions and goals which non-Christian counselors can't.

Can a Computer Help?

Can a task such as counseling which depends so profoundly on trusting relationships rather than techniques, and which is so person-centered, be assisted by computer technology? Isn't it an obvious contradiction to speak of the personal computer as a tool for the pastoral counselor? These questions point to an appropriate concern. It *is* possible to become mechanical and impersonal and thereby lose your effectiveness as a counselor. One pervasive characteristic of our age is impersonalism, the loss of individual identity. We all too often are considered nothing more than anonymous ciphers on somebody's printout.

In a hospital the other day, I heard one of the nurses say to her associates as she left the nursing station on that floor, "I've got to give 414 a bath." I don't know who the real flesh-and-blood individual was in room 414, but I'm sure he or she would take little comfort in such impersonal attention. We give our orders to disembodied voices electronically projected through a remote menu board at the fast food restaurant. We get our money from a computerized teller machine that cheerfully completes the transaction by saying, "Have a good day, Russell H. or Betty D. Dilday, Jr." Can automatic mechanized counseling, or worship, or prayer be far behind? The Bible places such importance on individual responsibility and worth, that we're reluctant to surrender personal tasks to a machine. Can a computer be used in counseling without surrendering this important personal quality?

In the Taoist tradition there's a story about Tsu-Gung, a disciple of Confucius.[5] Traveling near the Han River one day, he saw an old man working in his garden. He had dug an irrigation ditch, and descending into a well, the man would fetch up a vessel of water in his arms and pour it into the ditch. Even though he was working hard, the results were very meager. Tzu-Gung said, "There is a way whereby you can irrigate a hundred ditches in one day, and with little effort. Would you not like to hear of it?"

The gardener stood up, looked at him, and said, "And what would that be?"

Tzu-Gung replied, "You take a wooden lever, weighted at the back and light in front. In this way you can bring up water so quickly that it just gushes out. This is called a draw-well."

Then anger rose in the old man's face, and he said,

> I have heard my teacher say that whoever uses machines does all his work like a machine. He who does his work like a

> machine grows a heart like a machine, and he who carries the heart of a machine in his breast loses his simplicity. He who has lost his simplicity becomes unsure in the strivings of his soul. Uncertainty in the strivings of the soul is something which does not agree with honest sense. It is not that I do not know of such things, I am ashamed to use them.

That's a timely warning. It's possible to become mechanical and impersonal even in this, the most personal task the minister has to perform. But that can happen with or without the computer. Used sensibly, the personal computer can be an effective tool to improve your counseling ministry. In fact, increasing numbers of professional psychotherapists are already employing computers in their practices.

Examples of Computer Applications

A news article in *USA TODAY*[6] reported that DEC Rainbows, IBM PCs, and Apple IIes are taking over some tasks that once were the province of the psychiatrist or psychologist. You now stand a one-in-ten chance of running into a counselor that beeps at you, according to the article which quotes Yale University psychiatry professor Marc Schwartz.

"Computers are changing the face of therapy," says Schwartz, author of the recent book *Using Computers in Clinical Practice.* "They aid the psychologists in diagnosis, speed up appointments, and can often save the patient money." Here's how it works. You sit down at a personal computer in the counselor's office. It is programmed to ask you questions adapted from established psychological tests. Using what is called branching logic, the computer tailors a series of questions to each patient. For instance, if you say you're not married, it will focus the question on your life as a single person. The program can draw from a pool of thousands of questions.

When the test is completed, the machine analyzes your answers and pulls out the relevant research data that correspond to your answers. The result is a neat report on the "real you."

Another software program lets a patient sit at the machine for self-help exercises, such as an assertiveness training seminar. One psychologist says computers not only reduce the patients' bills by about 50 percent, but his clients tend to be more honest in answering questions with a computer. In one case, he says, a patient who flatly denied to him that she wanted to commit suicide revealed her true intentions to the computer. People feel like they aren't being judged when they answer to a machine, so they'll be more open. But doesn't the use of computers in therapy encourage a detached, noninvolved mechanical approach to what should be a very personal patient-counselor relationship?

"There will probably always be people who will misuse something like this, but in the hands of someone qualified, it can aid the patient and the doctor," says Bruce Duthie, president of Psychological Software Specialists, a software firm in Richland, Washington. Recognizing the potential for abuse, the American Psychiatric Association has plans in the near future to lay out some guidelines for computer use in psychology, according to the article.

So, acknowledging the limitations, there are some legitimate uses you can make of the computer in your counseling ministry. Already, a number of personality tests similar to the sophisticated version described in the newspaper article are available for use on personal computers. They could be helpful in pointing to certain strengths and weaknesses in a person's attitude and approach to life. Some of these tests require professional analyses that you may be unable to provide, but others have automatic assessments built into the program to help you interpret the results. Giving your counselee a computerized personality test won't begin to solve his problems, but it may provide a starting point in the early stages of the counseling process which Wayne Oates calls "The Relaxation and Rapport Phase."

As computer scientists and psychologists work together more closely, they will no doubt discover more effective applications to assist the counselor. We're still in the beginning stages of what could be a spectacular new advance in computer-assisted therapy. In Massachusetts experimentation in artificial intelligence is producing some surprising results already, as scientists try to develop what is called a fifth generation of computers.

In 1967 Joseph Seizenbaum, one of the scientists working on the project at MIT devised a computer program called "Eliza." It was designed to imitate a nondirective psychological interview. He did it as a joke to demonstrate the power of the computer, but also to poke fun at Carl Rogers's nondirective style of therapy. To his amazement, the program has been receiving glowing tributes as a serious tool, and has been hailed by some who took Eliza seriously as a breakthrough in psychotherapy.

Eliza begins its "therapy" session by inviting the counselee to type in a problem to which Eliza then responds with probing questions. The computer is programmed to key on certain vague or ambiguous words and comes back to the person with a demand for clarification, moving him to get in touch with what really troubles him. Eliza doesn't pretend to offer solutions, but rather allows the person to arrive at his own answers. The following is a sample of an actual counseling conversation between a patient and Eliza, the electronic therapist.

E. Hello, what's your problem?
I DON'T BELIEVE IN GOD.
E. Would you like to believe in God?
WHAT DO YOU THINK?
E. Would you prefer that I think yes?
CAN YOU HELP ME?
E. Do you wish that I help you?
YES.
E. How can I help you?

IS THERE A GOD?

E. Do you prefer that there is a God?

DO YOU?

E. Let's talk about you.

WHAT I REALLY WANT TO KNOW IS IF YOU CARE ABOUT ME.

E. Would you prefer that I care about you?

YES. (Pause)

E. Would you like to believe in God?[7]

The pause in the conversation is a dead give-away to the computer's limitations. When it receives a response it can't handle, it pauses to search its program for some question that will change the direction of the interview. Eliza doesn't have any idea what's going on with the person who questions it; it doesn't know what any of the words mean, or what the counselee is talking about. Obviously, enormous misunderstandings are possible.

Daniel Bobrow of MIT reports one such confusing experience with Eliza at their office. One Friday evening he had left a message on Eliza's screen that read "Type all messages into the computer and end them with a full stop." On Saturday morning a salesman showed up to try to sell some of the computer equipment they were developing. The salesman assumed that, as was often the case, the computer terminal was connected to Bobrow's home where he was monitoring the messages, so he began typing away, believing Bobrow would answer his inquiries. The following exchange resulted.

SALESMAN: Can I use one of the computers this morning?

COMPUTER: WHY DO YOU ASK?

S. I might be able to make some additional sales.

C. WHY AREN'T YOU SURE?

S. My prospective customers have never seen a demonstration of the system.

C. DOES THIS MEAN VERY MUCH TO YOU?

S. Of course it does.

C. YOU SEEM VERY POSITIVE ABOUT THAT.

S. This is ridiculous.
C. WHAT DO YOU MEAN THIS IS RIDICULOUS?
S. Is there any reason why I can't use a computer now?
C. TELL ME MORE ABOUT YOUR PROSPECTIVE CUSTOMERS.

The salesman had had enough by now, so he typed "Please dial me at 491-8150," which was the number of the telephone by the console. He was so mad, he forgot to end with a full stop, so the computer didn't answer. He sat there for a while, getting neither computer answer nor phone call. Finally, he called Bobrow at home on the phone, woke him out of a sound sleep, and said, "Why are you being so difficult?" Bobrow replied, "What do you mean, why am I being so difficult?"[8]

It's absurd to assume that a computer program could take the place of a counselor, but more absurd to realize how many people assumed Eliza was a serious program. But in spite of the absurdities and the misuse, there's a residue of serious development here that proves the computer has the potential to help you in your counseling tasks if properly used.

One pastor has a series of six premarital counseling lessons saved on disk which he loads on the screen, and revises to fit the particular needs of a couple he's counseling. In their first interview, he identifies what they need to work on, and in a matter of minutes he "tailors" the lessons to focus on those items. Then he prints out individual copies for the prospective bride and groom. He also uses the computer to personalize wedding ceremony instructions to include individualized directions for each member of the wedding party.

Another minister uses a filing program on his computer to keep track of resources (Scriptures, books, pamphlets, referrals) that apply to the various crises he encounters in counseling. He can call up his file on "drug abuse," for example, and find listed there a variety of helps accumulated over the years in dealing with teenagers in trouble. He even keeps a record of advice that has proven to be helpful in certain situations. When you're about to visit with couple "X" who are considering divorce, have you ever wished you could recall what you said to couple "Y" the other day in a similar situation? Couple "Y" told you later it was that statement with the Scripture passage you quoted that helped them start over. If you could just remember your advice it might help the two who are about to appear at your door. The computer helps you save and retrieve resources like that quickly and easily.

Keeping Counseling Records

The one element of your counseling task for which the computer can provide the most valuable assistance is record keeping. There are times, following a counseling session, when you'll want to write out a verbatim record that comes as nearly as possible to recalling everything that happened in the sequence of the conversation. Remember verbatims? You probably were required to write them during your supervised field work in the seminary. Or maybe it was when you signed up for Clinical Pastoral Education. Most CPE teachers ask their interns to write down following each counseling session a word-for-word account of what was said and done. The verbatim is then reviewed by the supervisor to pick out weaknesses and strengths in the interview and offer suggestions for improvements.

One of my responsibilities when I served as a Doctor of Ministry supervisor for Southern Seminary, was to require my degree candidates to turn in five verbatims which they wrote following real counseling situations in their churches. Before the students brought them to my office, they usually had reviewed the verbatims and had already picked out key elements which could be improved. It was an excellent training exercise to help a practicing minister become a better counselor.

Not necessarily after every session, but more often than not, I wrote verbatims of my counseling conversations and found the practice helped improve my ministry. Especially following controversial conversations, a detailed verbatim is very important in recalling what was said. There were other benefits, too. These written histories gave me a mechanism to checkup on my counseling style, besides being particularly helpful in reviewing data before the next counseling session with that same person. Because there were so many to keep up with, it was difficult to remember details of a counselee's life from session to session. But written verbatims kept me informed and helped me give more personal, detailed attention to those whom I tried to help.

Verbatim records are also useful when you have to refer one of your counselees to a doctor, a social agency, or to a psychologist or another pastor. It sometimes helps to send a resume of the person to the professional to whom you're making the referral. Since you want the letter to succinctly describe all the pertinent facts about the person's life and the process of your counseling sessions, the record you've kept is invaluable. You can then add to the factual resume your own interpretations and diagnoses. The verbatim notes you took will give greater accuracy to the letter and thereby help the one you write to pick up where you left off. When I had to make a referral, I was relieved when I'd kept full records and didn't have to rely on memory.

On other occasions there were appointments, routine in nature, that didn't seem to warrant a word-for-word record. But even after these, I always jotted some pertinent data to jog my memory the next time that person called for help.

If record *keeping* is important, record *protection* is even more important. Maintaining the confidentiality of counseling records has always been a recurring challenge. If you've been in the ministry very long, you know how many shocking secrets you discover in counseling that, if leaked, could cause irreparable damage. That fact always gave me a gnawing anxiety about confidentiality. So, short of writing in code or using lemon juice or milk for ink, I tried to devise ingenious schemes for protecting such sensitive data from the prying eyes of office personnel or visitors.

In my case, one guarantee of confidentiality was sort of "built-in." I wrote my notes in my own handwriting, which has never won a penmanship contest. Since my handwriting is as close to a secret code as human writing can get, that in itself was a barrier to unauthorized disclosure. But even with that protection, I always felt I needed to do more to ensure the secrecy of the records. Whenever I could, I used initials instead of names, filed the material in blank folders, and, then to be sure, I always kept them under lock and key.

You've probably devised your own schemes to keep your files secret. Because, not only must you satisfy your own anxieties about confidentiality, but the counselee's as well. If he knows records are being kept, he wants to be certain they'll never be revealed to anyone else.

This is one important job the personal computer can do for you better than anything else I've discovered. I wish they had appeared on the scene thirty years ago. For not only do they make it easier to record your verbatims and other counseling data, but they also can guarantee absolute confidentiality.

Let me illustrate how you could keep your counseling records on a TRS-80 Model 4P like the one I'm using to write this book. My word processing software is Radio Shack's SuperSCRIPSIT program which completely satisfies the requirements for serious writing. But it will let you do more than just write books, sermons, or letters. You can also compose and save brief notes, reminders, or any written material for that matter. I have one floppy disk on which I've saved an unlikely assortment of notes: "Mom's Social Security Data," "Poem at Robert's Wedding," "Helpful Hints from the Radio Shack People," "Ideas for Future Books," and a few others that aren't quite so profound. Some of these documents are only three or four typewritten lines in length.

If I want to look up what my Radio Shack friends told me on the phone the other day about a computer problem, I turn on my Model 4P, put the SuperSCRIPSIT disk in drive 0 and my miscellaneous data disk in drive 1, and push the reset button. When the hums and whirs stop, there on the screen appears a menu of options including, "Open a document." I select that one and type in "Helps," the name I gave my notes from Radio Shack. A few more hums and whirs and there it is on the screen, the customer service phone number at Radio Shack, the names of Doyle and Mindy, the service personnel who've helped me (and whom I've come to know like members of the family), and their advice from my last telephone conversation. Reading from the screen may be sufficient this time, or I may want a printed copy of my notes. If so, I just push the "control" key and the "P" key (that stands for "Print") at the same time, a print menu appears asking me to choose length of page, number of copies, etc. I make my choices, push the "enter" key, and, "rat-a-tat-tat," a perfect copy rolls out of the printer in thirty seconds flat! (I still get emotional when I see this crazy machine work!)

Now, do you see how that same technique could be used in keeping counseling notes? Let's take an imaginary case. Mrs. Edith Jason has made an appointment to see you this afternoon at 2:30. After church last Sunday she mentioned her problem briefly to you in what might be called a "pre-counseling" conversation, so you have a pretty good idea what she wants to talk about. Her husband's been drinking heavily and showing other signs of stress, and she wonders what's troubling him and what she ought to do about it. Since your membership records are stored on the personal computer at your office, you call up the Jason family file and see that Ray, Mrs. Jason's husband, is a salesman for a computer company that has been on the brink of bankruptcy for six months. They have two girls, twelve and fifteen. They've been married eighteen years and have moved six times during those years. It's already easy to see some patterns emerging that will help you understand more quickly Ray's symptoms of stress.

Now, slide your SuperSCRIPSIT word processing program

(or a similar program you may be using) into the disk drive slot on your computer. Push the reset button and load the program. Select the "Open a Document" option from the menu and fill in the data. You're asked to name the file, so let's call this one "Jason." You may assign any name to a document you wish within these limitations: you cannot use more than eight characters, you cannot use a numeral as the first character, you may add a three-character extension to the name by typing in a slash. That means you could name your file: "Jason,Ed/Ray," for example.

Now we're ready to take the step which allows you to protect the confidentiality of your notes. My program does it by allowing you to add to your file name an eight-character password to limit access to the file. Be creative. Pick out any password you like. Use the name of the county where you were born, "Potter," or your wife's maiden name, "Doyen," or a biblical name like "Tertius." (You remember, he was the "Word Processor" Paul used to write his Letter to the Romans. Only they called them amanuenses in those days.) Just choose some term that isn't obvious, but one you can easily remember. Type a period after your document name and then add your password, like this: "Jason,Ed/Ray.Tertius."

Next, push the "enter" key, and the computer records the name of your document, seals it with your password, and then offers you a blank page to write anything you wish. Type in the data from the Jason's membership records which will help you remember this family, along with your own impressions of what may be the trouble. When you're finished, push the "control" key and the "Q" key (that stands for "Quit," you know, like "To quit a document.") at the same time, and the document is automatically saved on the disk.

Just for fun, let's test the security of your data. Go back to "Open a document" again and type in "Jason,Ed/Ray" and push "enter." After a few hums and whirs, a message appears: "File Access Denied." You have to enter the password. Try again, but this time type in the password which no one knows but you: "Jason,Ed/Ray.Tertius." This time the information you wrote about the Jasons appears on the screen in a flash.

I know this security system works. Short of overhauling the entire program, there's no way of getting around a password on a document. One day, after naming a file, I accidently added a password without realizing it. Apparently, after putting a period after the file name, I accidently touched a key or two without noticing. I didn't realize the computer (dumb machine) would think those characters I accidently typed in were a password. Since I can't remember what I added to the name (dumb machine owner), I still can't get into that file! I've tried every combination I can think of, and the Model 4P hums and whirs and says, "File Access Denied." I even reminded my machine that I'm its owner, and that I might trade it in on an IBM if it didn't cooperate, but to no avail. The password system is inviolate!

Now it's 3:30 and Edith Jason has left. It was a good counseling session. You established a trusting relationship and encouraged her to express her feelings and describe her anxieties about Ray. She did, and it's obvious there are deeper problems than his drinking. So, she plans to come back Friday for another appointment to explore some possible factors in their marriage that may be causing Ray's symptoms. Now, while the conversation's fresh on your mind, load up your computer, use your password to call up the Jason document, and type in a verbatim of your conversation with Edith. It'll take only a minute, and you can correct, change, and enlarge it easily until it's just right. Push "control" and "Q" and the new information, added to the old, is saved on the disk behind your password. It's ready for your review next Friday before Edith comes in. You can rest assured no one else can see it accidently or even if they tried to pry. You and Tertius know the material is secure.

By the way, don't leave your password written on a note pad, or taped on the side of your desk. You do have to use common sense in keeping it secret. Of course, should you carelessly leave it lying around one day, or for some other reason you're not sure your password is safe, just make up another one, change the name on your document, and it's secure again.

If you'd rather not use a word processing program to store your records from counseling sessions, and prefer instead to keep brief factual data on your counselees, you can use a filing program like PFS:FILE. The space for detailed information is limited but may be sufficient for your purposes. Using a file program has one advantage over a word processing program: you can search and manipulate the data on any number of counselees. This is particularly helpful if you want to do research on various trends or factors among a large list of counselees.

One minister keeps a record according to the problem each counselee raises. He uses 3 x 5 cards, but a computer filing system would work better. First, he labels an index tab with each of the major complaints he's dealt with over the years:

1. Alcoholism
2. Drug abuse
3. Divorce
4. Mental illness
5. Religious doubts
6. Parent-child conflict
7. Sexual maladjustment
8. Vocational decisions
9. Church group tensions
10. Church membership decisions
11. Personal salvation
12. Spiritual welfare of relative or friend

He adds others as time goes along. After each counseling contact, this minister puts the person's name and notes of the conference on a card and files it behind the appropriate tab. Sometimes several of these concerns surface in one person, so he tries to determine the dominant, overruling difficulty that person is facing. Reviewing the file for statistical trends gives the minister an accurate awareness of prevailing needs in the congregation and helps him plan his preaching and new ministries for his people. Having all the notes on various persons filed by categories allows him to build a data bank of helps he's used over the years as new people come to him with similar complaints. PFS:FILE would be an excellent tool for creating and managing this type of counseling file. A similar password system can be used on these files, too. Put a period after the file name and add any password you wish. No one can retrieve the information but you or whoever knows your password.

Learning to Do It Yourself

This might be a good time to comment about the importance of learning to use the computer yourself, rather than depending on a secretary. There are, of course, duties that ought to be delegated to staff members, freeing you to work at ministry tasks, but operating your personal computer is not one of them. Lots of people are having to change long-standing ideas about executive types using a machine. Up to now, it's been considered imprudent for a manager, an officer with the company, or, in your case, a minister, to do their own typing. That's still true in most cases. Your time is valuable and is best used when you let others who are skilled and trained help you. But in this new information age, using the keyboard of a computer is another matter altogether. More and more, that keyboard is your only access to information, and there are many times when it's quicker, wiser, and more accurate for you to use it yourself without going through someone else.

In the chapter on sermon preparation, for example, I tried to make it clear that the old classic method of preparing sermons, with handwritten study notes, rough drafts, dictation, retyped copies, corrections, and final copy, can be vastly streamlined by your own use of a word processor. Once you try preparing sermons on a computer, I believe you'll agree doing it yourself is better. But this chapter on counseling presents other advantages so convincing, I think I can rest my case. In this chapter, the primary reason for doing it yourself is that the confidentiality of counseling records requires it. There's no other way. Either you write them out tediously by hand, and then struggle, as I did, with ways to hide, disguise, and lock up your notes to protect them, or you can let a trusted secretary do it for you. Choose the second option and the bond of confidentiality is broken, no matter how trusted your secretary may be. Since it's preferable to write and store counseling records yourself, why not do it the easiest and most efficient way?

So, get out the old high school typing class notes, or buy a book, or take a course. Or—wouldn't you know it—the computer can teach you to type. I have a program called Typing Tutor that leads you through a series of lessons, and then monitors practice sessions by checking your speed and accuracy. You'll be exchanging your "hunt and peck" method for the quicker "touch method" in no time.

Remember those advertisements for piano lessons that used to appear in comic books? They pictured an unlikely wallflower moving toward the keyboard of a piano after having taken the mail-order lessons that secretly have turned him into a virtuoso. An unbelieving crowd watches him, assuming he knows nothing about pianos. The unforgettable line under the picture is, "They all began to laugh when he sat down at the piano."

Take a few typing lessons, practice regularly, and who knows, you may dazzle *your* friends too. Can't you picture it: you casually move across the office floor toward the "mysterious" complexity of a personal computer. The crowd watching you is intimidated by computers. They wouldn't even know how to turn one on. But to their amazement, you confidently sit down at the keyboard. And the caption reads: "They all began to laugh when he sat down at the computer!" Then, you'll be glad you learned to do it yourself.

The personal computer and pastoral counseling may appear to be unlikely partners. Mechanical precision and a warm, person-centered ministry may sound mutually exclusive. But my contention is that a caring shepherd can maintain his sensitive concern for his flock while, at the same time, sharpening the precision and the skill of his shepherding. Use common sense. Maintain spiritual balance and equilibrium. Don't become a digital counselor who spends more time fiddling with gadgets than helping people. But on the other hand, don't ignore or reject mechanical devices that can help you, and thereby let the contributions of technology benefit only the secular world.

Martin Luther's philosophy of music was, "Don't let the devil have all the good tunes." We could say, "Don't let the devil have all the good machines." The computer may be a providential gift from God to expand and improve your work —especially the work our Lord had in mind when He taught us to care for His sheep.

Notes

1. C. W. Brister, *Pastoral Care in the Church* (New York: Harper & Row, 1964), p. 167.
2. See Brister, pp. 175-76.
3. Wayne E. Oates, *The Christian Pastor* (Philadelphia: Westminister Press, 1951), pp. 116-138.
4. Oates, p. 178.
5. From "The Machine as Technique," *Epiphany,* Vol. 4, #1, Fall 1983, p. 24.
6. *USA TODAY,* April 5, 1984, p. 3B.
7. "The Machine as Technique," p. 123.
8. See *Psychology Today,* May 1983, p. 58.

6
The Personal Computer and the Minister's Records and Calendar

Whether we like it or not, our lives have gradually become electronically ordered. Evidences of this ordered environment are everywhere, but one startling description of it appeared in an article by Richard Coniff in *Next* magazine entitled "Bid Privacy Farewell." Coniff describes how the life of an average student at Baylor University is controlled by the computer.[1]

> Every time Sarah Donnelly visits one of the cafeterias on the Waco, Texas campus of Baylor University, she hands the cashier an identification card showing her name, photo and Social Security number. A terminal connected to a central computer reads a magnetic strip on the back of the card, confirms that Donnelly is up-to-date in her meal plan payments and makes a note in the computer's memory next to her number: "Meal eaten."

The article then traces Sarah Donnelly's steps around the computerized campus. At the library, the I.D. card lets her through the turnstiles, automatically checks out the books she chooses, and makes a note of them in the computer's memory. If she stops at the campus bookstore, unless it alerts the clerk that she's behind on payments, the same card charges her purchases.

Next, is the health center where she must hand over the card for admission. If she hasn't paid her health fee, the computer blocks her at the door with the tactless message: "Denied." The same scenario takes place at the school marina and at the swimming pool. Finally, if Donnelly wants to attend a football game, she presents the card so the box office can verify by the computer that she's a full-time, paid-up student entitled to a free ticket.

It's all very efficient, and one would have to be paranoid to read ominous implications into the system, but there's something about such electronic ordering that troubles us. It wouldn't happen at Baylor, certainly, but couldn't such a system, designed for efficient record keeping, also be used for social control? An unscrupulous university could survey the information it accumulates on the students to determine who *isn't* attending football games, what books the students are reading, which meals they're skipping, or how often a student buys a certain prescription or seeks treatment at the health center. In fact, such a computer system could lend itself to a kind of "on-line" surveillance, logging the whereabouts of individuals, and, by denying them access to various functions, turn a "troublesome" student into an instant nonperson on campus.

Coniff warns that misuse of the computer as a surveillance tool isn't as farfetched as we might think. It could happen to any of us, whether or not we're on a college campus. If it's not possible already, some day the computer will be able to locate you instantly, twenty-four hours a day, every time your various credit card and identification numbers run through a computer—at a restaurant, an automatic bank teller, an airline ticket machine, or a hotel. Shades of George Orwell! That's carrying an ordered lifestyle too far.

Hopefully, our American society will not allow such blatant abuses, but even at best our lives will always be subjected to continuing electronic ordering. Just now, as I type these words, my electronic calculator/alarm clock, tucked away in my briefcase on the table, sounds its distinctive chime: three tones marking the last three seconds of the preceding sixty minutes, and a louder tone, one octave higher, to mark the hour. Even if you wanted to, it would be difficult to escape those electronic cadences which constantly surround us, calling us to get organized.

That's not all bad. Who hasn't learned the proven advantages of time management, careful scheduling, and a prudent stewardship of the calendar? Everyone knows that careful record keeping can save time and increase professional efficiency by ordering the data with which we work. So don't let your fears of a creeping Orwellian society cause you to reject valid applications of the computer in bringing order to your ministry.

Ministerial Records

The scientific environment within which most of us have grown up encourages us to quantify everything. Statistics translated into graphs and charts seem to have such innate authority that a numerical report showing a 10 percent growth in anything impresses us. Unfortunately, this pervasive tendency toward quantification has invaded the ministry. How many pastors, ministers of education, or ministers of music do you know who measure the success of their work on the basis of numbers?

I can remember associational missionaries who at the annual meeting in October would vindicate the worthwhileness of their position by reporting the number of phone calls made, cards and letters mailed, churches visited, sermons delivered, and miles traveled. Some of these denominational servants had the clever ability to accent their statistics with certain vocal inflections that always drew "oohs" and "aahs" from the messengers attending the associational meeting; especially when they reported on the "miles traveled" category.

With a humility that seemed out of place when marching his statistical accomplishments before us, one missionary always spoke in the third person, "In carrying out his heavy responsibilities, your missionary has driven this month—(He paused, looked up at the people as if to say, 'You're not going to believe this,' then glanced back at the notes to prove he wanted to be accurate.)—3,296 miles!" Reporting it that way not only guaranteed congregational "oohs" and "aahs," but usually brought forth an outright gasp or two. Numerical statistics always impress us, and, even in the ministry, we've adopted the tacky habit of showing our worth and measuring our success by quantification. Especially during the last few years which have witnessed the rise of "super churches."

Our models of success in the ministry today are pastors and other ministerial professionals who serve these notable gigantic congregations. We assume they must be doing it right, or the results wouldn't be so fantastic. Examine the numbers. Check the graphs. Since the results *are* fantastic, and since they *must* be doing it right, they become patterns for the rest of us to copy. Well, certainly we can learn from those whose numerical successes are so obvious, but quantified statistics are not the *only* success indicators of quality ministry. If they were, then Jesus himself could not be considered a success, and therefore not a likely model for ministry today. There are other criteria for measuring success in ministry, and I hope our denomination will develop a whole new set of "quality indicators" before we degenerate into the idolatry of number worship.

Yes, I know numbers are important. Numbers represent persons, and persons are the ultimate focus of our work. The minister who loses sight of that fact and dismisses record keeping altogether as incompatible with genuine ministry is as far off the road on one side as the statistical-minded minister is on the other. Balance—that's the secret. What we need is a balanced, healthy attention to records. For even though they're not the exclusive gauges by which we measure progress in ministry, records are *one* gauge, and an important one at that.

Let's talk about the pastor's record keeping first. While most seminaries try to provide practical courses in how to be a pastor, not many offer classes in pastoral bookkeeping. Since maintaining records is not the most exciting part of your work (some would say it's the dreariest), you probably wouldn't be inclined to sign up for such a course, even if there were one. So, never having been taught how to do it, most pastors put together some system of record keeping on their own, or else they adapt a method they've seen another pastor using.

What records should a pastor keep? When I began my first pastorate, someone solemnly warned me that records of weddings, baptisms, and funerals were important because lawyers, judges, and other unnamed important governmental officials were always asking pastors to verify these data for legal reasons. With equal solemnity I believed them, and from my first week in the ministry I've kept careful records of weddings, baptisms, and funerals. But I've been doing it for thirty-two years now and have yet to receive a request from any legal professional for my data.

One time a member of our church, whose company was sending him to Saudi Arabia for two years, required verification that he was a "Baptized Christian," and since I had immersed him five years earlier, I had the "awesome" responsibility of going back through my records and authenticating his baptism. Even though I'm still waiting for that first legal inquiry from an important government official, I am nevertheless convinced that a pastor ought to keep such information. The only way you can remember wedding anniversaries, stop by a home a year after a father died, analyze the ages of those you've baptized, and countless other things is by keeping good records.

During my second year as pastor in Antelope, Texas, my first church, having tried several different formats for pastoral record keeping, I discovered a book called *Pastor's Five-Year Record Book,* developed by W. Ross Edwards. I bought a copy, and have used it with satisfaction these thirty years. It's a spiral notebook about 5 x 8 inches, divided into eleven sections:

Biography Weddings

Funerals	Sermons
Addresses	Mid-Week Messages
Revivals	Churches Served
Articles Published	Occupational Expenses
Miscellaneous (Will, Insurance, Etc.)	

Some of the categories were not much help in my case, and there was no section to record baptisms, but having no need to keep occupational expenses in this book, I crossed out that title and relabeled the section, "Baptisms." With that slight modification, the book has served me well.

However, if I were starting out today, I would find some way to afford a computer and would enthusiastically put technology to work keeping my records. Although as a seminary president, my record-keeping needs have changed, I've already made the switch from *The Pastor's Five-Year Record Book* to PFS:FILE on my personal computer. It's as much an improvement over the old way as an electric typewriter is over a quill pen. Were I still keeping pastoral records on baptisms, weddings, and funerals, the advantages would be even more impressive.

Using my own system as an example, here's how you can make an easy transition from notebook records to a computer. My book included pages for 209 weddings in five years, about two a week, nearly one-third more than I needed in even my "marryingest" five-year period, including a few romantic leap years. The form itself is adequate and provides space for the groom's name, age, address, telephone, church membership, and parents; the same for the bride; the place and date of the wedding; license information; fee; address after marriage; and comments. But 209 is too many forms for most pastors and a large section of each book is wasted space. Since the form is sufficient, and since I've been using it for several years, I've chosen the easy way to transfer information from the book by duplicating the form on the computer. No need to waste time and effort creating a new one.

One of the most popular filing programs today is PFS:FILE with editions for most popular computers. No doubt one reason for its popularity is that, unlike so many others, this program's instruction manual is clearly written with abundant step-by-step illustrations in each chapter, making it easy to learn. PFS:FILE is "menu-driven," which means you don't have to memorize a long list of procedures. Instead, menus are printed on the screen from which you are invited to select the next procedure. In computer jargon, that's "user-friendly." (I suppose computer enthusiasts speak of cafeteria lines as menu driven and user-friendly, too.)

After a few minutes of orientation with the manual, switch on your computer, load the program, and then just follow the steps as the menus move you from one procedure to the other. You'll be using the system like a pro in a short time. As an illustration of how you could employ a computer filing system to manage your wedding records, here's how you'd do it with PFS:FILE on my computer. Any other system you choose would be very similar.

Ready? Insert the PFS:FILE program disk in drive 0 and an empty floppy disk for your data in drive 1, and push the reset button. Sure enough, as promised, there on the screen is the "Main Menu." In its natural, user-friendly manner it presents you with the following choices:

1 DESIGN FILE	5 PRINT
2 ADD	6 REMOVE
3 COPY	7 EXIT PFS:FILE
4 SEARCH/UPDATE	

SELECTION NUMBER:
FILE NAME:

Choice number 1 enables you to create a new file form or change one you've already created. With function number 2, you insert the data in the proper places on the forms. Use number 3 to make duplicate copies of forms or files. Once the data is stored in the files, you can retrieve them in various ways with function number 4, and print out the material by choosing number 5. Number 6 lets you erase selected information, and function number 7 is the way you leave the program before turning off the computer.

Since you're just beginning your computerized wedding file, move the cursor to the position just beyond the colon following SELECTION NUMBER, and type in the number "1." Beside the colon on the next line where it says FILE NAME, type the name you want to give your file. Let's use "Weddings."

Granted, it's not a very innovative name, but you'll have to admit it is descriptive. Now push the Fl key on your computer keyboard, and the program executes your choice and brings you the DESIGN FILE function. Just as you expected, there on the screen is another menu, this one with only two choices:

1 CREATE FILE
2 CHANGE DESIGN
SELECTION NUMBER:

See how easy this is? Since you're getting used to these multiple choices by now, be bold and make your decision. Number 1 describes best what you want to do, so type in that number as your selection and push the Fl key again. PFS:FILE gives you a blank page on the screen so you can design any file form you want. Remember, we were going to save time by simply duplicating the wedding form in the record book without having to be creative, so move the cursor around the blank page and type it exactly as it is in the book.

GROOM: AGE:
ADDRESS: TELEPHONE:
CHURCH MEMBERSHIP:
PARENT'S NAME AND ADDRESS:

BRIDE: AGE:
ADDRESS: TELEPHONE:
CHURCH MEMBERSHIP:

PARENT'S NAME AND ADDRESS:
ADDRESS AFTER MARRIAGE:
PLACE OF WEDDING: DATE:
LICENSE—COUNTY: STATE: FEE:
COMMENTS:

That was easy. This form only asks for nineteen items, and each one will require only a line or two of space, so the entire form fits on the screen easily and can be stored three forms to a page. But, just in case you need it, PFS:FILE allows you to make each form as long as thirty-two pages with a maximum of 100 items on each form. That would be a world-class form! And it will surely give you all the flexibility you could possibly need. Since the wedding form you've just designed (or rather, copied from the book) is relatively small, you can probably record all the weddings you will ever perform (about 450) on one floppy disk. For practical purposes, however, you'll probably want to keep a separate disk file for the weddings in each church you serve.

If the form on the screen looks all right to you, store it by pressing the Fl key again which takes you back to the main menu. Now select function number 2, ADD, so you can begin to record data on the blanks forms. As you complete each record, the ADD function keeps giving you empty forms, one by one, until you've filed every wedding.

Up until now, I've been pressing you to learn to operate all the computer programs yourself, and this one also can be easily handled by the pastor. But, this is one computerized record-keeping task you could delegate. If you're fortunate enough to have secretarial help, use it here, but stay familiar with the system so you can manipulate the files yourself if you desire.

Whether you or your secretary enters the data on the form, there are some suggested guidelines to follow, such as: always enter last names first, and enter dates with two characters for each part of the date. (For example, May 7, 1984 would be entered: 84/05/07.) As you complete one form another empty one comes up on the screen until you're through transferring all the wedding data from the record book to the computer's memory. Then, after your next wedding, use the same ADD function to enter the information on a new wedding form, and you're up-to-date.

Now that your wedding records are all on the disk, is this system really any better than the book? Indeed it is. And the next function will prove it. Go back to the main menu and select function number 4, SEARCH/UPDATE, which immediately presents you with one of your blank wedding file forms. Although it looks like the same screen you used to fill out a form, this one is different. To be sure you know it's different, the program labels it RETRIEVE SPEC. Just move the cursor to any one of the nineteen items on the blank form and type in whatever information you want to find. For example if you want to call up the file on the Dawson wedding, type in the name "Dawson" beside the GROOM blank on the form, press the Fl key, and in a second, the Dawson wedding information is before you.

Or, for a real demonstration of the computer's ability, try this. Suppose you want to know how many weddings you've performed for brides who were younger than twenty-one. Move the cursor to the AGE blank on the form and type in, "<21." That "<" symbol means "less than," and the computer knows you want to see all the wedding files where the bride is less than twenty-one years of age. Touch the Fl key, give the machine a second or two, and one by one, the weddings with young brides will be listed on the screen. After you've reviewed each file, the computer gives you a summary of how many files it examined and how many it found in the category you requested.

Do you want to know Mrs. Dawson's maiden name, or where the Dawsons moved after they married, or how many of your weddings last year were performed for nonmembers, or how many were performed in the sanctuary, in your study, or at home? Any combination of information you'd like to retrieve can come to you instantly as long as you included it correctly on your form.

If you want to, you can protect your new wedding file with a password, but since the information really isn't confidential, there's no need. It is wise, however, periodically to make a backup copy of your files on another floppy disk. The operating system of your computer makes this a simple procedure using the BACKUP command. Even though they're amazing devices, computers aren't perfect. Accidents do happen, and it's possible to lose information. A backup is good insurance.

While we're on the subject of weddings, here's another helpful suggestion. Why not file your wedding ceremony on a disk using your word processing program? When you sit down with the couple to go over the ceremony, print out copies of a "generic version" for the three of you to review together, and discuss any changes they might want to make.

Have you noticed more individuality in wedding ceremonies today? Some couples want to use the "unity candle," some have one ring, others two. Some intersperse the ceremony with music. One couple may want you to add a special Scripture or poem, or the bride may want to include some vows her mother used in her wedding. Seldom can you use a simple, standard ceremony without some tailor-made adjustments to fit a couple's special requests. That's no problem as long as their suggestions don't violate your convictions or the church's policies about what ought or ought not to be included. Once the three of you have agreed, just make the changes on the screen, add their full names instead of the blanks most copies have, and print out three perfect, individualized ceremonies, one for each of you.

When I look at the yellowing wedding ceremony notes clipped in my Bible, with dozens of penciled changes making it almost illegible, and with eraser-worn holes where names ought to be, and when I compare those notes to the clean individualized copy just described, it almost makes me wish

I were starting over again so I could put the computer to work in my ministry. (Notice, I said, "almost.")

Let's turn now from the "wedding" section to the "funeral" records. This section of my five-year record book is a grim reminder of the pastor's role as a comforter. At no other time are you able to be as effective as a spokesman of God's Word than in being with people when a loved one dies. Looking back over the records of the last few years of my pastoral experience makes me glad I filed the information. If for no other reason, the data calls to mind some people, now with the Lord, who meant a great deal to me and to our church.

There's the man who, more than any other single individual, was responsible for implementing my dream for the church's television ministry; on the next page there's the retarded son of a famous evangelist; on another the oldest member of our congregation, who remembered so much about the early days. Then there's the couple, married for fifty years, who died just four days apart; our church hostess; the mother of a teenager who now is a seminary professor; and the brother of my fishing partner.

When I recorded the information about the funeral of Mrs. Arthur Rutledge in October 1977, who would have predicted that, within a few days, I would fill in the next form on the page with the information about the death of her husband, Dr. Rutledge, the executive secretary of our Home Mission Board, and one of my heroes? Each record tells a story, and seems to say, "Lest we forget."

Sentimental reminiscence is one, but not the primary, reason a pastor ought to keep funeral records. My wife Betty still remembers how her pastor, Dr. Boyd Hunt, came by her home the first Christmas day after her father died. It was a thoughtful gesture of pastoral concern, reminding the family that God cared for them and the church did, too. Even a brief note one year after the death of a spouse or a parent can mean so much to a grieving family, but good timing in such contacts depends on accurate records.

The same advantages you get from computerizing your wedding records can be applied to funeral records, too. In fact, you can repeat the same procedures outlined above, including the duplicating of the record form in the book. Just name this file "Funerals" instead of weddings. In addition to the factual data about the deceased, the form in my record book calls for data on cause of death, place of interment, Scriptures used in the memorial service, and who made arrangements for the funeral.

Using such a form, with its search and retrieval capability, PFS:FILE enables you to research your data to find an impressive variety of facts: the leading cause of death in your church membership; trends in where memorial services are held—church, funeral chapel, graveside, or home; and the most appropriate Scripture passages to use in the death of little children, suicides, accidents, or other unique situations. Having such information readily available in any form or fashion, knowing it's accurate, and being able to print error-free copies of it in a few seconds, makes the transition to a computer worthwhile.

Build a "Baptisms" file next, and you'll have most of your pastoral records covered. Name, age, date, address, and parents' name are the only categories I've kept up with in baptismal records. But knowing the computer's power to retrieve facts from files, you might like to add certain items such as: a code to determine how this person was led to Christ, whether or not the person came from another denomination, or a record of other family members who made professions of faith later. Over the years it would be valuable to verify from this hard data the relative importance in a person's salvation experience of Sunday School membership, parental influence, a pastoral visit, the sermon, or the witness of a friend. Pull together that kind of research with your new computer file, and you're better prepared to recommend an evangelism plan for your church.

Whether you're just starting out in the ministry or have

thirty years of handwritten notes in a five-year record book, putting pastoral care records of weddings, funerals, and baptisms on a computer filing system makes sense. But if I were asked which of my records were the most important in terms of everyday use, I would have to answer: preaching records.

That's the section in each of my five-year books that's easily located because of its threadbare pages. It shows the wear of a thousand fingerprints and the stain of a hundred coffee cups. Nowhere else can you see accumulated in one place, the evidence of the blood, sweat, and tears of a lifetime of ministry than in the record of sermons preached on Sunday; Bible studies, and devotionals brought in mid-week services; addresses delivered, and messages used in revivals. Under every other section of my record book, there are blank pages. But not in the preaching sections. Every line of every Sunday and Wednesday are filled in from beginning to end.

That's where the emphasis ought to be, isn't it? For preaching the Word of God is your highest calling. You may spend enormous chunks of time witnessing, counseling, visiting, consoling, and administering, but the preparation and delivery of sermons should always receive your highest attention. As president of the largest seminary in the world, I've given up most of the duties I spent my life addressing as a pastor except one: preaching. I still think of myself primarily as a Baptist preacher. God called me first of all to preach, and I'll never get away from that call, even though my time is directed toward institutional leadership and management.

Will the computer keep better records of your sermons? By now you know my answer is an enthusiastic yes! For years, I've kept sermon notes filed consecutively from the first one preached to the latest one a few Sundays ago. Each sermon, address, or mid-week message is given a number, starting with number 1 years ago to the last one, number 2025. So, in my record book, along with the ready-made blanks for date, subject, text, and place, I had to add another column for sermon numbers.

Employing function number 1 in the PFS:FILE program, I've designed a new form that not only adds a place for the number, but also separates subject from title, divides text into Old Testament and New Testament, and adds a blank to list whether the sermon is one of a series of messages. Now locating sermons by number, text, subject, or date is so much easier. Besides, I can now research the data to determine how many sermons I've preached from the Old Testament as compared to the New, which biblical books I may have overlooked in my preaching plan, or whether I'm riding a hobbyhorse by spending too much time on a favorite theme.

Using the old form in the book, if I wanted to find the sermons I had preached from the Book of James, or on the subject of repentance, for example, I had to slowly run my finger down the text or subject column until I found one, make a note of it, and keep looking. It was slow, and I was never sure I hadn't overlooked one. Or if I wanted to look up that "great" sermon I preached a few years ago on "Humility," but I couldn't remember the exact title or text, I would have to use the same page-by-page process. Now PFS:FILE lets me select the search function from the menu, type in the word *humility,* and it finds the record instantly, giving me text, title, number, and all the other information on the form.

Similar data can be stored for mid-week messages, addresses delivered at the PTA, Rotary Club, or pastor's conference, devotionals, lectures, and Bible studies. Your revival records are also easily managed by the computer. If all you can remember is that you held a revival meeting in Shelby, North Carolina, but the date, pastor, and what you preached have been forgotten, no problem. Load your program; call for a search; beside the blank for "location" on your screen type in the word *Shelby,* and the full record is before you, even if it was fifteen years ago.

Review the chapter on "The Personal Computer and Preaching" to see how using a word processor to write and store sermon manuscripts, teamed up with your new filing system, can give you the best possible combination for managing your preaching ministry.

You've probably already thought of a dozen other records you could improve by using a personal computer. I just thought of a couple myself. Why not store your vocational resume on a word processing disk so that it can be quickly updated and sent out when you get publicity requests? You could even have a long form and a shorter one for different uses. (Maybe the 150-page capacity of a floppy disk would be enough space for the shorter, humble edition.) Tax records, reimbursable expenses—there are other records you could file, some of which will be discussed in the chapter on the personal computer and the minister's family.

If you're a minister of music, this entire section can be applied to keeping records of choir members, anthems, special oratorios or dramas, or your own repertoire of solos. The same procedures are also applicable for ministers of youth, education, or any other of the growing number of specialized ministries in the contemporary church.

Maybe "revolutionize" is too strong a verb, but it comes close to expressing accurately what a computer can do to your record keeping style—especially in a day which places such a high premium on orderly work.

Ministerial Calendaring

They're in a desk drawer bound together by a rubber band —seventeen little blue shirt pocket calendars printed by the Baptist General Convention of Texas and distributed each year to pastors and other ministers in the state. For seventeen years of my ministry this little blue book was my official appointment calendar. It listed important denominational dates and left tiny blanks for each day, on which I added tiny notations about engagements. Since my schedule wasn't very demanding in those early years, it was sufficient. Now those seventeen blue rubber-banded booklets are a sentimental record of a significant portion of my life. There's another packet of similar calendars in the same drawer that belonged to my father. It never dawned on me until recently that I had copied his system of date keeping. But comparing the two stacks of calendars reminds me that he influenced my ministry in more ways than I realize.

When we moved to Atlanta, I changed to another calendaring method, exchanging the pocket calendars for a multiyear desk calendar that opened to a full month of activities. Using the large calendar, Nancy Morgan, the efficient assistant with whom I've worked for about fifteen years, has developed a fail-safe technique to keep me on schedule, even though the calendar has become more complex year by year. She refuses to let that master desk calendar out of her sight. Without it, my ordered existence would become a disaster, so she makes machine copies for my own desk and for my home.

From the "sacred" desk record, she types the detailed schedule for each day on a 3 x 5 card. I carry several weeks of these daily cards in my pocket to keep me on time for appointments. The cards are big enough to record data such as directions to a church, which airline terminal my flight leaves from, the name of the person who invited me to speak, or the reason a certain person is coming to see me. Each day Miss Morgan updates, adds to, and drops cards for my pocket to keep the schedule current. So that's my three-tiered calendar system: handwritten desk calendar which is the final authority; current copies on my desk and at home; and a supply of cards in my pocket.

Despite my enthusiasm for the computer, we'll probably keep this system in place rather than replace it with a computerized version any time soon. However, we have yielded to several enhancements made possible by electronic technology. For one thing, the typed record for my pocket cards is now stored on the computer so that when a new stack of cards is needed, it's relatively easy to make the changes and print out new ones.

Some day, when our office has a network of computers in place enabling the same data to be called up on several screens at once, we'll probably shift to a computer calendar program. There are several good ones available with advantageous features that make them preferable to old-fashioned systems. One of these programs is installed in the TRS-80 Model 100 briefcase computer and is sufficiently representative to serve as an illustration.

Since it's built-in, you don't have to insert disks, or design forms; it's ready to use when you flip on the switch. The small screen comes alive with a menu of programs, including the Schedule program, and you select it by pointing to it with the cursor and touching the "enter" key. It's very simple, but at the same time, sophisticated enough to do the job.

From my desk calendar I transfer to the Model 100 those appointments that are not routine, listing them by month, day, and hour. There's enough room to include details about the engagements, and you can enter an entire year of dates in no time. Every day or two, I spend a few minutes updating the calendar by adding new dates, changing existing entries when necessary, and deleting the reminders no longer needed. Since the Model 100 goes with me on trips, I always have my basic calendar for an entire year in a form that makes it remarkably accessible. By that I mean you can do some things with a computer calendar that are impossible or at least very difficult to do with the paper kind.

For example, when I enter the schedule program on the Model 100, I can push a key labeled "find," type in any word or number in the calendar data, and the computer will find it. Type in "commencement" and immediately the dates of our three annual seminary commencement exercises appear on the screen along with information about rehearsals, speakers, and so forth. Not only does the Model 100 list these three, it brings up also the commencement exercise where I'm to bring the address next May in North Carolina. That's an extra bonus.

Suppose I want to know how many open Sundays I have this year without a preaching responsibility. Since I've entered these with the designation, "Sunday Hold," I simply push the "find" key, type in "Sunday Hold," and the computer lists all of them. Maybe I've agreed to lead the Bible Study for a state convention meeting in the fall, but I can't remember where or when. Ask the Model 100 to find a reference to "Bible Study" in the calendar, and it will list several, one of which is bound to be the date I'm searching for. Furthermore, it will show the entire month of April, or let you slowly scroll through the entire year. In a computer package no bigger than a three-ring notebook, this program, along with four others, gives you enormous flexibility in managing your work.

Ministerial record keeping and calendaring has come a long way in this modern age of electronic life ordering. Just how far is graphically illustrated when you read Andrew Blackwood's classic book *Pastoral Work.* In his chapter entitled "The Habit of Keeping Records," he advises:

> For keeping membership records, one can use cards, preferably four by six inches. When purchased by the hundred, they are not costly. In preparing to make calls, it is easy to take out certain cards and put them in the pastor's notebook. This book he carries in his left side pocket. . . .
>
> When the pastor moves into another parish, what should he do with these records? He may well leave his successor the lists of members. As for most of the other records, they should be kept. A hundred cards weigh only half a pound and fill only an inch of space in the files. At the next parsonage they can be put on a remote shelf, there to repose until needed.[2]

That antiquated advice does show how far we've advanced in the techniques of record keeping, but a few paragraphs later, in the same book, he gives some timely counsel that shows we may not have come far enough in the philosophy of record keeping:

Let the minister never use these records as a basis for boasting. Not even in a farewell sermon should this sort of self-glory prove needful. Why recount the number of calls he has made and his other numerical achievements? Whether or not the dear man means to boast, he should have something more worthy of such a vital occasion. No man can bear witness to Christ and to himself at the same time. In a farewell sermon why not dwell more largely on the book of The Acts, with its message of divine power, than in the book of Numbers with its human statistics?[3]

Notes

1. Richard Coniff, "Bid Privacy Farewell," *Next*, July/August 1981.
2. Andrew Blackwood, *Pastoral Work* (Grand Rapids, Mich.: Baker Book House, 1945), p. 128.
3. Blackwood, p. 129.

7
The Personal Computer as a Church Management Tool

Using the computer as a church management tool is not a new idea. Fifteen years ago, the church where I was pastor took the "revolutionary" step of computerizing its membership and contribution records. Gathering the original data on each member was a tedious process, but it allowed us to have printouts of members according to age, residence, profession, interest, and former experiences in church jobs. Since we did not have a computer in the church office (not many did in those days), we contracted with a local insurance company in the city to handle our processing for us. Once a month, offering envelopes, now emptied by the money counters but still bearing the name, number, and amount of the contribution, were bundled up and delivered to the insurance company office. There, the information was transferred to the computer files from which, once a quarter, the contribution record of each family was printed and mailed. We also received a copy at the church office for answering inquiries.

Granted, it was a primitive process, but this was before the computer revolution had started. Some churches may still send out their records for computer companies or "service bureaus" to manage; a few may share data processing with other churches (sometimes called "computer consortia"); but such arrangements are no longer typical. The ecclesiastic computer scene has changed dramatically.

For one thing, more churches now own and operate their own computer systems. Hard on the heels of that trend is a corresponding proliferation of companies selling programs and equipment designed exclusively for churches. Tracking them is a mushrooming network of organizations for church computer users (such as The Southern Baptist Computer Users Association), and following them a spate of magazine articles and books about computers and the church. It's a technological/ecclesiological snowball that gets larger as it gathers momentum.

Another change in church computer use is the shift from larger business systems to the more flexible, affordable personal computer. In order to meet their complex needs, some super churches may install micro or mainframe computer systems with multiple terminals and enormous capacities. But most churches will be better served with quality personal computers. Even large congregations, installing several compatible units in various offices, may find the personal computer a better investment.

That's the direction most colleges and universities seem to be going. A few years ago, any discussion of computers on the campus would have encouraged the purchase of a large central computer not only to meet the traditional data processing needs of the school, but to serve the individual needs of faculty and staff offices too. But now computer strategies in most universities are changing. Instead of enlarging the number of terminals, thereby expanding the accessibility of their central mainframes, colleges are adopting a more flexible strategy. They're buying personal computers which can, if necessary, access the mainframe. For example, Rice University recently announced it had joined the twenty-four-school "Apple University Consortium," which includes such institutions as Yale, Carnegie-Mellon, Columbia, Cornell, Princeton, Dartmouth, and Notre Dame. Over a period of three years, each school agreed to spend two million dollars for Apple personal computers and software at 50 percent discounts in exchange for university experimentation and research. The resulting research data is shared with the Apple company and the other member schools in the consortium.

The size, speed, sophistication, and serviceability of the personal computer have improved so impressively they can now hold their own with the larger business computers. Since, even with these added improvements, the prices continue to fall, the personal computer is clearly the choice of the future, not only for universities, but for churches, too.

Always alert to these trends, the marketplace is scrambling to produce church-related programs for use on the popular brands of personal computers. I have a current list of such programs that includes: church management and Bible learning programs for the Apple II, plus thirty church programs for CP/M computers such as Digital, four programs for the Franklin Ace 1000, scores of programs sold by seven companies for IBM PCs and XTs, two companies that offer twenty-two church programs for the TRS-80, and on and on. The personal computer in church is an idea whose time has come, and a congregation without a computer in a few years will be like one without an electric typewriter now.

Here's a list of possible tasks a personal computer can perform efficiently in a typical church office:

Membership records
Visitation support
Personnel records
Voluntary talent and skills inventory
Church archives
Safeguarding confidentiality of records
Word processing
Mailing lists/directories
Master calendar and scheduling
Correspondence log
Committee reports
Standardizing administration procedures
Accounting and budgeting

Stewardship records
Pastor's and staff calendar/appointment/expense records
Sunday School attendance analyses
Church music inventory
Preparing order of worship service
Weekly newsletters
Energy control
Physical security
Teaching and training
Church library records
Inventory of materials
Computer conferencing
Electronic mail
Data bank searches
Research and statistical analyses

There are others, of course, and an alert minister can discover new applications or learn how to improve existing programs by "picking the brains" of business personnel in the church membership who work in computerized offices. Since the efficiency needed in their offices is no different from the efficiency needed in yours, many of their business applications can be easily adapted to the church. As a church administrator, you should be just as well organized as the administrator of a successful commercial enterprise. Actually, you ought to be better, since you have a superior mission. Doesn't the Bible say we are to be as wise as serpents and as harmless as doves (see Matt. 10:16)? Now I'm not suggesting that the secular business people in your church are the serpents you should be as wise as, but you certainly can take lessons from them without losing your "harmlessness."

If, however, you're not too good at technical creativity, if adapting the computer programs deacon Smith uses at his hardware store doesn't appeal to you, you still have a way to computerize your church's business functions. The number of packaged computer systems for churches is growing. Multiplying would be a better word for what's happening; and they're not only getting more numerous, they're getting better, too. Let's examine some of them in greater detail.

Examples of Packaged Programs

The Sunday School Board of the Southern Baptist Convention sells a complete computer system that addresses most of the administrative tasks a church must perform. It's called Church Information System. While it uses minicomputers, a category just above the personal computer classification, it will be helpful to review it briefly. Using the Data General Desktop Generation hardware, the system allows several desktop terminals and printers to work from the same central processing unit. This flexibility lets the church tailor its system to its size by purchasing only the units it needs. Eight software programs designed particularly for the larger church are a part of the package.

1. *A membership program* builds a master file of information about members and prospects, efficiently provides either selected reports (by sex, age, class, etc.) or churchwide listings for a variety of purposes. Simply touch a few keys and print out master membership lists, mailing labels, directories, Sunday School class rolls, prospect files, family profile sheets, or committee worksheets.

2. *A word processing program* assists in formatting, compiling, and editing letters and other typewritten material. Not only can you prepare bulletins, newsletters, and reports more quickly, but with greater accuracy and quality as well.

3. *A general ledger package* supports the church's accounting and financial reporting needs. When financial transactions, including receipts, deposits, disbursements, and journal data, are entered on the terminal screen, they're automatically posted and processed. Do you need to create a tailor-made financial report for your church? One feature of this package lets you customize your reports to fit the distinctive preferences and financial needs of your church.

4. *A stewardship package* keeps track of individual pledges and contributions. Each member's record is established in the system with an initial entry of that person's pledge amount and frequency (annually, monthly, or weekly). Thereafter, contributions are recorded on a weekly basis or as received. A history file is maintained for one year, from which printed reports can be prepared on request.

Other programs include accounts payable, payroll, prospect visitation file, and attendance tracking. CIS also advertises a full range of service and maintenance options from the manufacturer of the equipment and from the Sunday School Board, including training and telephone inquiries when problems are encountered.

Another supplier has designed a system to operate on an Apple III computer.[1] It comes with ten software programs.

1. *Church Membership Master System.* Information on each member, entered in the record once, becomes the basis for the other programs in the package. From this master list, the church office can retrieve information such as birthdays, professions of faith, schools attended, or a list of persons who live in a certain neighborhood. First names (even nicknames) and appropriate salutations can be inserted for mailing labels or visitation lists. With just the push of a button, an accurate copy-ready membership directory can be printed from this master file in a matter of minutes.

2. *Church Office System.* This program includes word processing with suggested formats for bulletins, newsletters, and other frequently printed materials. It allows you to send personalized letters to selected individuals in a fraction of the time it would take to type each one separately. There is even an electronic dictionary with a church-related vocabulary that automatically checks the spelling in your documents. And, on top of all that, you can add to the dictionary those words that may be unique to your denomination. (Lottie Moon and Annie Armstrong probably will not appear in a dictionary or in electronic spelling-checkers either.)

3. *Church Talent and Organization Package.* Use this program to keep track of committees, ministry teams, choirs, deacons, or other groups. It can tell you the talents, interests, and past experience in church work of each member, and you can search and list the information by any categories you desire.

4. *Church Attendance Package.* With this feature you can monitor attendance in Sunday School and worship services. Absentee patterns are traced so that teachers and staff members can be alerted to visit those who may be dropping out.

5. *Church Donor Package.* This program records pledges and their current status, prepares reports to be sent to church members, and helps you customize the system to your church with as many fund categories as you like. Envelope numbers are not needed since the records are personalized by name. A password security system preserves confidentiality.

6. *Church Financial Package.* Keep records of church budgets, income, expenses, payroll, debt retirement, and other typical financial data with this accounting package. When checks are written, they are automatically deducted from appropriate ledger accounts. Financial spreadsheets, one of the most popular business applications for computers, let you display and easily change data to create "what-if" situations for planning. Suppose you are submitting a building program proposal to members for their approval. The spreadsheet gives you "hard data" projections of the capital available to the church if each family increased its pledge by a certain percentage and if the membership grew by a certain amount. Sure, any ten-dollar calculator can do that, but the spreadsheet lets you enter a number of other factors, and instantly, all the columns of figures are automatically recalculated to give the picture of each changing situation. It's a great tool for planning.

7. *Pastoral Care Package.* This program makes it easy to keep track of members who are in the hospitals, sick at home, shut-in, or who have other special problems. Information on persons who are recently divorced, single parents, foster par-

ents, or physically handicapped are maintained and can be listed by categories. A privacy code ensures that only the minister or other approved persons have access to this information.

8. *Church Study Package.* Survey designs are provided to let a local church poll its members for their opinions about worship services, program needs, church property, mission outreach, and a number of other concerns. (If you're courageous and secure, you can even find out what they think of your sermons.) An updated data base of information on typical churches around the country is maintained so you can compare your church with others. The program also helps you analyze your collected data and print reports.

9. *Church Leader Package.* This package uses the computer as a self-learning instrument and offers orientation courses for Sunday school teachers, committee chairpersons, and other leaders. It gives programmed instruction on leadership styles, decision making, how to organize a group, how to have a good meeting, teaching methods, and other subjects. You can also add material to meet the unique leadership training needs in your own church.

10. *Christian Education Software.* Self-teaching lessons such as "An Overview of the Bible" and "Bible Facts" provide learning opportunities for all ages. Suggestions are given for individual or class use.

The company that produces this church system promises to update its customers, provide training, answer questions, and maintain a network of up-to-date information free of charge for the first two years. Each month a new disk of helpful information is mailed to the church. Excerpts can be transferred from the disk directly to your computer for inclusion in newsletters, bulletins, sermons, or fund-raising appeals.

Another "turnkey" system includes the usual programs for accounting, word processing, stewardship records, and other office functions, but specializes in church growth applications.[2] The computer's ability to quickly manage information is linked to the various laws of church growth to help a congregation reach people. How does it work? The following illustrations are given as examples.

1. One of the laws of growth is that most people come to Christ and join the church because of the influence of relatives and friends. It follows, then, that the best prospects the church has are the acquaintances and relatives of its members. Research indicates that the average church member can identify about eight unchurched people, who, according to this law, are the ones most likely to respond to outreach efforts. When information about this "potential congregation" is placed in the computer, the church can analyze its needs, design programs to meet those needs, and thereby more readily bring them into its fellowship. A special outreach program comes with the package to accomplish this.

2. A second law is that most people join the church after having first attended as a visitor. These are the prospects with an obvious interest in the church, and, if they visit several times, they are highly receptive to joining. A contact from the church soon after their visits has proven to be an important factor in their decision to join—but not just any kind of contact. If it is a generic, institutional contact, only 8 percent come back to visit again; if it is a personal contact, 30 to 50 percent return. So, a program has been designed to implement this law. It suggests the following strategy: Mrs. Smith visits the church. She's a widow, works in a bank, and likes jogging and tennis. The computer program identifies three church members about her age, who are also widows and who are interested in the same sports. One of them happens to be a bank employee, too. The minister asks them to call on Mrs. Smith, new friendships are formed, and Mrs. Smith is encouraged to join the church.

3. Another law of church growth says that new members continue in the church if their needs are being met and if they are properly integrated into church life. A program in this package monitors members' talents, skills, and interests so

they can be enlisted to serve where they're needed. Not only is the ministry of the church expanded in this way, but the members become happily involved doing what they like to do, and are therefore more committed to continued church membership.

4. Fourth is the law of preventing and reclaiming dropouts. Effectiveness depends on tracking member participation records for signs of deteriorating attendance, and then taking quick action to contact them before their absenteeism becomes chronic. The first stage in the dropout pattern is a noticeable decline in church activity. The person may attend worship only once or twice a month, may still give financially, but begins to drop other activities. The second stage is a worsening record. Worship attendance drops to once or twice a year, stewardship deteriorates to a token amount, and there is no contact otherwise except for special days such as Easter, weddings, and funerals. The third stage is total dropout. The person is still on the roll, but does not attend, give, or participate. Usually, when people change their patterns of church attendance, they may be calling for help; they may feel no one cares. But if you respond immediately, at the first sign of trouble, you let them know you care and want to help. If the church knows about the potential dropouts' changing pattern of activity and has a strategy for contacting them, these inactive members can be brought back. One program in this computer package flags those with patterns of irregular attendance, giving, or participation in time to let the church take action.

"The Ministry Enhancer" is the ambitious but interesting name the manufacturers give this church computer package. The name is a pretty good definition of the computer's role in church administration. Computers don't take the place of a caring, personal ministry, but they can enhance the efficiency and expand the capacities of your work in the church.

"Sure," you say, "that's all well and good for a large, multistaff church, but I'm pastor of a small congregation where I'm the *only* full-time employee. Can all this new technology help me?" Yes! In fact, the personal computer just might be a greater enhancer of your work than it is for a pastor with a team of staff specialists.

A major percentage of the pastor's work, especially in a smaller church, is "administrivia"—routine tasks that are important, but time-consuming. When you have a staff of assistants, these details can be shared or delegated; but when you're the only one, or when your help is limited, these repetitive jobs have to be done by "you know who." My contention is that while the computer has the capacity to handle the complex work of a large church, it really performs at its best for ministers like you.

Picture the following scenario: you're the pastor of a small-town church with 250 members, many of whom you constantly call on for leadership tasks in the church's programs. Since you enlist them so frequently for volunteer service, you hesitate to ask for their time in less important, mundane duties, so you end up doing those yourself.

There's the monthly newsletter, for example. It seemed like a good idea last year when you launched this new publication, and it's been well-received by the members, but the deadline for mailing it comes around so regularly. It's not the most fulfilling function of your ministry to type out the copy and paste it together for printing. And, occasionally, in the midst of this frustrating duty, you've even been known to ask, "Who's idea was this, anyhow?" Not only is there no one there to answer your question, but there's also no one else to blame. It was your idea, and it was a good one. But isn't it a shame humans have to perform tasks that are so mechanical? Since there's no one to answer that question either, let me respond. Yes, it is a shame, but there is a solution. You guessed it, the personal computer.

Put away those fragile stencils and that messy blue correction fluid. Push aside the typewriter with its unforgiving keyboard. Turn on the computer, load your word processing program, and type out the first draft of the articles, news items, and reports you'd like to include in this month's issue. Since the few errors you make can be corrected easily, you don't flinch every time you strike the wrong key. You say you'd rather have the article about the Easter sunrise service printed at the top of the first page across both columns? No problem. Touch the correct keys and the entire section is positioned where you want it. Besides that, you can instantly center any text you please, underline or double-strike for emphasis, change type styles, and justify the right margins for a very professional touch. The copy never looked better. Your computer printer will type out a perfect stencil, or a stencil can be made directly from the computer copy. Before you know it, in far less time and with far better quality, you're finished.

Now for the step you dislike even more: addressing the paper to the various families and individuals on your mailing list. First, the mailing list has to be updated. There are a dozen addresses that have to be changed, and you suspect that even as you correct the list, there are, unknown to you, moving vans backing up to other houses to relocate other families and play havoc with your list. There is nothing more certain than that following the updating of a mailing list and the addressing of a church paper, somebody will move. This recurring frustration can be relieved by the computer, because the mailing lists can be changed or enlarged with so little effort. Then, push a button on the computer keyboard and print a perfect string of up-to-date labels; and again, in much less time, you're ready for the next job.

Very likely you're also the one who must prepare each Sunday's bulletin. Can you imagine how much easier that job would be when the basic order of service is stored on the computer? Unless you want to revise the entire worship format, all you need to do is pull up the bulletin form from the disk where you saved it, change hymn numbers, Scripture references, special music, and sermon title, and you're ready to print out a perfect copy for reproduction. Embarrassing typographical errors? Not on your computer's life. What a relief to know that Sunday morning you won't see the teenagers laughing because your finger missed the "g" in typing the hymn title, "Come, Christians, Join and Sin."

Then there are those form letters you usually mimeograph using that impersonal salutation, "Dear Member." Now they can be stored on a computer disk, personalized, and sent out to "Dear Bob and Mary." It doesn't take any longer, and the letters are warmer and more personal than the mimeographed variety. Of course, computerized letters can become "too professional," and, if you don't monitor the process, even the computer can get things crossed up and make an occasional mistake. I received a computerized letter the other day addressed to "Dr. Russell Baptist, president of Southwestern Dilday Theological Seminary." It began, "Dear Dr. Baptist!" It sounded like I had really moved up the "denominational ladder!" It also sounded like it came from a machine and not a person.

With little or no secretarial help, a pastor can use the computer to provide daily lists of people who have birthdays, who joined one year ago, who lost a spouse a year ago, who are about to have a golden wedding anniversary, or who have reached an age when they might be ready to make a profession of faith. Your telephone call or personal visit to them is more effective because you were there at the right moment. One pastor has a prayer time in the worship service during which those with birthdays the past week are lifted up to the Father in intercession. To be remembered in prayer by one's church family is a meaningful experience; and if you weren't in church the Sunday your name was called, it's also a very effective motivator for future attendance.

Whether you're pastor of a large First Church or a small congregation in the suburbs or the village, the personal computer can help you with the administrative functions of your ministry. Equipment and programs are getting better and easier to use, and new applications for church usage are appearing every month. For example, the pastor of a small Congregational Church in Connecticut uses his Commodore 64 personal computer as an electronic bulletin board. It sits atop an old pulpit against a wall in the church foyer on Sunday and scrolls across its screen the latest church news and announcements. A thirteen-year-old computer whiz in the congregation programs the news each Friday and even adds animated cartoon characters and computer-generated music to capture the church members' attention.

Greg Belin, Business Administrator at Second Baptist Church in Houston, Texas, has developed several unique computer applications for a large church. In a recent letter he said:

> I am working on a Radio/TV module right now to help keep up with our viewing audience. It will tell us who and where our viewers are, what stations they watch or hear our program on, and track their contributions (which aren't a lot because we ask them to send them to their local church). We can use this to analyze the effectiveness of our air-time dollars that we are spending and help us locate our best market areas. These programs will also keep up with our incoming mail and tell us the status of this mail. By indicating what topics we want to address in our return letter, the system will compose that letter from text already stored in the system and merge in the person's name and contribution amount to produce a personalized response. The system will also track the pastor's book and cassette tape orders and print the cassette tape and mailing labels, as well as a packing list for our mail room to use in shipping these out.

Greg is also working on a program for their school which will automate class scheduling, attendance, and grade reporting.

New developments in the field of computer-assisted instruction are also beginning to have an impact on church educational programs. As an illustration, a firm in California has a program for the Apple II personal computer called

Doctrinal Texts System. Aimed at teenagers and adults, this educational program teaches doctrine by leading the student through key theological passages in the Bible. It has graphics, sound effects, and corrective cues. The same company sells Catechetical System for mastery of Luther's Catechism. There are Bible tests which total your score as you answer questions, and a number of other programs that make Bible learning fun for children.

Mormons are using computers in the work of their temples and in their local congregations.

> Computers have helped automate record keeping in the temples. They help draft plans for new church buildings. They index 70,000,000 names for the International Genealogical Index. They alert bishops when ward members are eligible for baptism or ordination. They typeset magazines and materials for Church members. They keep track of membership records, read and record financial documents listing donations by ward members, and help with translation of Church materials into seventy-two languages. They even plot patterns for temple clothes and then cut them out. And these marvelous instruments are doing much, much more.[3]

> The *Atlanta Constitution* called the Atlanta temple a "space-age marvel of electronics," referring to computer systems in the temple. Magnetically coded plastic computer cards identify the patron and his or her ward as that person enters the temple. Later, that same card is used to record the name of the proxy as ordinances are performed. Through the use of computers for ordinance work, hours of time and labor that once took place in the baptismal office are now reduced to ten or fifteen minutes per baptismal session. Sealers and baptismal font recorders can record ordinances with the push of one button. Endowment sessions no longer require four typists and four stake checkers. Reports on the number of ordinances done monthly by members of each stake in a temple district can be compiled in five minutes rather than three or four

hours. And 11 1/2 tons of paperwork each year have been eliminated.[4]

A Dallas inventor has even designed an electronic prayer guide for Muslims. A small computer points the way toward Mecca from any of 200 locations, beeps at worship time, and displays the opening verses of the call to prayer on its liquid-crystal display screen. To use the device, travelers press a button to enter the name of a city they're visiting. The computer does the rest. It seems the merging of science and religion knows no geographic or cultural bounds![5]

Rabbi Irving Rosenbaum is head of the Institute for Computers in Jewish Life. This Chicago-based organization helps plan the use of technology in Jewish religious practices in the United States. In addition to some computer games such as "The Philistine Ploy" and "Samson and Delilah," Rosenbaum described some other very serious applications. There is a computer program for the Apple II which generates Hebrew letters so the computer can use the Hebrew language. There is also a program that runs through the steps of the Passover Seder ritual and even a kosher cookbook called *Jewish Compu-chef.* There's also the huge *Responsa Data Base* which has been developed in conjunction with Israel's Bar-Llan University. This electronic library contains 38,000 documents of Jewish custom and law dating back several thousand years. Talmudic scholars can consult this data base to shed the light of the ages on modern dilemmas. When a question is raised, the data base in a matter of seconds can search 600 million bytes of information and produce the related citations.

A Catholic publishing house in California is producing computerized catechisms under the title *In Christ Jesus: Testing Program and Computerized Inventory.* A Chicago-based corporation is producing computer programs for the Indian Sikh religion. It contains Sikh scripture passages, dietary and nutritional information, as well as 2,000 Yoga exercises practiced by the sect.[6] It seems almost every branch of religion in the world is beginning to apply the computer's power to its particular faith.

For church musicians, the personal computer is providing an increasing number of programs that assist them in composing original music. Radio Shack sells inexpensive software that lets even nonmusicians compose tunes that will then be written out and played in various synthesized tones. While Bill Gaither and Buryl Red will probably not be threatened by a new wave of competition, the computer does open up the possibility of creative compositions from ordinary musicians in the congregation.

Where can you get information about programs for your church that will work on your computer? The best source is recent issues of religious magazines such as *The Christian Ministry, Eternity, Church Management, Church Administration, Christianity Today, Christian Herald,* and others. The computer stores in your community will have lists of programs that work on their machines, and most denominational offices offer suggestions too.

While it's not a substitute for hard work, prayer, or effective leadership, the personal computer can be a valuable new tool to help you. Just as the carpenter can justify using a power saw, the CPA a calculator, or the farmer a tractor, so the minister is justified in employing the best tools possible in performing with excellence the work God has called him to do. And the possibilities of *this* new tool are staggering. In fact, the Great Commission might well be fulfilled in our generation if God continues to supply remarkable tools like the computer to help us with His work. But what if we hesitate or refuse to employ these new possibilities? The potential for failure is staggering, too. We need bold vision and courageous innovation to match the possibilities God has providentially placed at our disposal.

When someone says, "We don't need a computer in the church." Your answer could be, "You're right. And we don't need air-conditioning, vacuum cleaners, typewriters, adding machines, projectors, tape recorders, maps, and books either, but they sure do help."

Notes

1. The supplier is Adam Church Management System in Champaign, Illinois.
2. Insight Church Software is described in *Church Growth: America,* Spring 1983, p. 5.
3. "The Church and Computers," *The Ensign,* June 1984, p. 24.
4. "The Church and Computers," pp. 25-26.
5. *Time,* April 2, 1984.
6. Phoebe Hoban, "Church on a Chip," *Omni,* June 1984, pp. 40*ff.*

8
The Minister's Computer and Electronic Networking

Southern Baptists have taken what appears to be a gigantic step in simultaneously launching two nationwide electronic networks within a few days of each other; the ACTS television network and the Baptist Telecommunication Network. Looking back years hence, we'll probably see it was really a baby step into a fledgling technology, but to us now it's a gigantic step which we suspect will alter our lives considerably. Not even our boldest visionaries can predict what the impact of this giant step into electronic networking will be. The ACTS television network, sponsored by the Southern Baptist Radio and Television Commission, is already greatly enhancing our evangelistic efforts by allowing us to preach the gospel to millions of homes across America and around the world. But it's the Sunday School Board's Telecommunication Network that concerns us here as we discuss the possibilities of linking churches together for exchange of information.

Employing the latest satellite technology, the Board has begun a network that will link together every association of churches in the Convention and eventually the churches themselves. Giant receiving dishes called "downlinks" are being installed in the yards of churches in many places. These huge saucers are precisely aimed at a satellite floating hundreds of miles in space in order to receive the messages which it relays from the Board's headquarters in Nashville, Tennessee. For years, the normal method of sending information from the denomination to the churches was to print and mail it, or to film and deliver it in the form of movies, videotapes, or filmstrips. But today that same information is being instantly transmitted over the network directly to the churches for live viewing, or for taping for later use.

Smaller churches, unable to afford the necessary equipment, can receive the information through their associational office. So for the first time, churches are being linked together in an electronic network that could radically alter the way Southern Baptists make decisions and carry on their cooperative enterprises. Already live telecasts of annual Convention sessions are being sent to the churches across the nation. Conceivably in the future, there would be no need to have expensive Convention meetings in distant cities for church representatives. Instead, members of the congregations could gather in their own auditoriums. There, before a television screen, each church could simultaneously hear proposals, make suggestions, and vote its convictions on issues, without any of its members having to leave town.

While most of the material being transmitted by BTN is in the form of television instructional programs, the satellite network could also be employed as a vehicle for transmitting printed data from the Sunday School Board's giant computer to personal computers in the churches and vice versa. In 1981 CompuServe information service and Warner Qube television cable company conducted a successful experiment to connect personal computers in user's homes to the CompuServe computer in Ohio by means of the cable system, totally bypassing telephone circuits. This feature could become the most valuable application of the Sunday School Board's network in the future, and points to the remarkable capability of the personal computer to exchange data with another computer to which it is connected. In computer jargon, this is called "networking." And it isn't necessary to have a satellite in order to do it. Computers can talk to each other over regular telephone circuits.

Everyone became aware of the possibility of linking two

computers when the movie *War Games* was released, with its frightening story of a high school student who breaks into the national security computer and nearly sets off World War III. At about the same time, there were several widely publicized legal cases involving teenage computer geniuses who breached the electronic security of large computers. They were able to access the information kept in the mainframes of a number of government agencies, hospitals, and businesses. While they apparently did little damage, the nation suddenly became alarmed at the possibilities of computer crime by means of networking. It was natural, therefore, for many people to associate computer linkups with unsavory circumstances.

Admittedly, there is the possibility of abuse. But isn't that true of any new technological development? Unredeemed humanity will inevitably find a way to express its sinful nature by means of the latest innovations of science. It is already possible for computer networks to be used to organize political groups within a denomination. With data banks of names, addresses, and phone numbers, and with the capability for instant communication which the computer allows, information can be sent proposing a candidate for election to a leadership position just before an annual meeting. Strategies for blocking actions or suggestions about how to vote on certain issues can be quickly disseminated before an upcoming denominational meeting. In this way someone could build a power base to influence important decisions.

But in spite of the potential for abuse, the good outweighs the bad, and informational networking is here to stay. It has the potential for improving relationships between churches, ministers, members, and institutional leaders within a denomination. In fact, computer networking is one of the fastest growing uses of the personal computer today.

Computer Networking

Networks have been described as the connections that make us one people on one small planet near one small star. They are, at the same time, our newest and our oldest social invention. John Naisbitt defines networking as people talking to each other—sharing ideas, information, and resources. He points out that networking is a verb, not a noun. The important part is not the network, the finished product, but the process of communication itself. One of his "megatrends" is a predicted change from hierarchies of pyramid-like organizations to a multiplicity of small "networks" of people around common interests. Networking can be carried on through conferences, phone calls, air travel, books, papers, pamphlets, photocopying, lectures, workshops, parties, grapevines, mutual friends, summit meetings, coalitions, tapes, newsletters, and now, of course, through computers.[1]

With the exception of the two-way radio, there have been few opportunities for the public to participate directly in broad-based communications activities until the arrival of the personal computer. Now, through computer networks, there is the possibility of "many-to-many" communication unlike anything man has known before. Sociologist Elaine B. Kerr in her book *Computer-Mediated Communication: Status and Evaluation* says that computer networks facilitate human group communication among geographically dispersed people that is faster and cheaper than the alternatives—by letter or phone or travel. They can serve purposes as homey as swapping recipes or as serious as doing research or holding on-line conferences. One computer "meeting" on the future of education in Florida lasted from February 7 to April 3, 1980. Sixty-six participants from across the state and from as far away as Washington, D.C. exchanged data and opinions using personal computers linked over the telephone circuits.

The use of computers to bring a small group of people together for exchange of specific information is only one manifestation of networking. Other networks are general in nature and are open to the public. There are over 1,300 data bases, 500 free computerized bulletin boards, and scores of national information services available to the personal computer user. Some computer owners are enthusiastic travelers through this "network nation." In lieu of luggage, these travelers are equipped with terminals, communications software packages, modems, telephones, and cables to connect the two. In place of plane fare, they purchase connect time. They explore the networks' broad range of subjects in order to meet new friends, discuss current issues, find information, and, in the case of Christian groups, engage in electronic witnessing.

I don't really understand it, but every bit of information you put into a computer can be converted into sounds which can in turn be transmitted at lightning speeds over ordinary telephone circuits. A page of double-spaced text can be sent from one computer to another in about thirteen seconds. A 100-page report takes about twenty minutes. Because of its speed and accuracy, "telecomputing," as it's called, is preferable to mail or to ordinary telephone calls when it comes to sending detailed information. The computer also produces better quality copies of the data than is possible with telephone facsimile machines.

In order to link two or more computers together for this kind of data exchange, each one must be equipped with a device known as a "modem." That's shorthand for modulator-demodulator, technical terms for the conversion of electric impulses into sounds and back. It would be much simpler to call it a computer-telephone connector, but whoever makes up computer jargon likes to maintain a sense of mystery about high tech in order to dazzle the uninitiated. So the connecting device you need is called a modem. They come in two varieties. Acoustical modems are connected to the computer and have a cradle with two round receptacles onto which you place the ear and mouth pieces of your telephone handset.

Direct-connect modems, as the name implies, plug directly into the computer on one end and the telephone on the other, without having to involve the handset at all. This latter type gives a better connection and is therefore more expensive. Modems also come in two speeds: 30 and 120 characters per second. Since that way of describing their respective speeds is too mundane and easy to understand, the jargon creators have provided us another way: they speak of 300 and 1200 baud. As you might expect, the faster one is more expensive.

You must also have a software program which controls the transmissions. Some computers supply them as built-in features. But there are a number of inexpensive software packages from which to choose. Once you have a program and a modem, the sources to which you can connect your computer are innumerable. There are commercial information services such as CompuServe and THE SOURCE. Electronic bulletin boards specializing in every conceivable interest from cooking to scuba diving can be called up for information. (See *The Computer Phone Book* referred to in the chapter on preaching.) Libraries, bibliographic services, stock market reports, airline ticket reservations, banking services, on-line shopping catalogs are only a few, and this list doesn't come close to exhausting the choices. Two people can also connect their computers together to talk to each other, or they may share information using an electronic mail service offered by one of the commercial information services.

Using the same modem and software, you can also connect your personal computer to a mainframe computer in a remote location and operate it as though it were a terminal in the mainframe system. I've already tried this by sending material I've written on my Model 4P directly to the IBM Displaywriter in my office to be put into final form by a skilled operator on our staff.

Telecommuting

Connecting a personal computer to an office mainframe has opened up the possibility of certain employees being able to work at home instead of driving each day to the office. In *The Third Wave,* Toffler predicted thousands would be working at home in what he called "electronic cottages" with their computers connected to their company mainframes. Rather than spending valuable hours fighting freeway traffic, valuable money on office clothing, and valuable capital on parking places, telecommuters would start their work while others were crawling along the turnpike, sit at their home terminal in inexpensive blue jeans, and leave the car in the garage. Besides saving company overhead, productivity rises from 20 to 60 percent among telecommuters. They tend to work more hours, face fewer distractions, pace their work to their style, and have no compulsion to "pack it up" at the end of the day to catch the 5:08 train home.[2]

Toffler prophesied that our biggest factories and office towers might in our lifetimes stand half empty, reduced to use as ghostly warehouses or converted into living space. Telecommuting hasn't yet caught on to that extent. The reason, Naisbitt explained, is that paralleling "high tech," there has developed a simultaneous desire for personal relationships which he calls "high touch." People want to be with other people, so working at home away from other people hasn't had the sweeping appeal that Toffler saw. Nevertheless, there are about seven million personal computer users who work from their homes in the United States.[3]

Furthering this remarkable growth are some unique applications of telecommunications which are being tested. For example, Best Western International in Phoenix has set up a remote computer site in a woman's prison in order to employ the inmates to handle their reservations system. American Express has designed a work-at-home program especially for the handicapped.

There are also some unusual developments which illustrate the impact telecommuting has had on society. First, in their book *Working from Home,* Paul and Sarah Edwards deal with the special problems of working at home, such as how to resist robbing the refrigerator all day long and gaining weight, or how to deal with the strain working at home can place on a marriage. A whole new family of social problems has been born as a result of this new technology.

Second, the AFL/CIO recently passed a resolution banning computer homework except for the handicapped. The unions are concerned that people working at home on "piecework," might be tempted to put their children to work on their home terminals and perhaps double their output. This could cause employers to require more work from their employees without more pay, and could lead to child labor abuses.

Third, real estate developers are investing millions of dollars in an "electronic village" called Eagle Crest in California. Each of the 360 homes is being equipped with computer facilities which will link the homes via telephone lines or microwave with computers anywhere in the world. The houses will have computer-based home management systems and networks which let neighbors have electronic garage sales and bulletin boards. Eagle Crest is being promoted for professionals interested in telecommuting.

While it may not catch on so rapidly that Toffler's vision of empty office buildings will become a reality, society can't ignore the impact computer networking will have on our lives.

Ministers serving in the midst of the computer revolution must not ignore the impact either. If the trend continues, the families you'll be called upon to serve in the next decade will not necessarily be the typical nine-to-five families which most of our churches are organized to reach. We will need some creative approaches in ministry and evangelism proposed by innovative ministers who are not afraid to meet changing conditions with new ideas.

Networking and the Minister's Work

But its impact on the people you're working with is not our only concern. Networking may affect your own personal working patterns, too. Most of networking's effect on your ministry will develop in the not-too-distant future. We're not far from being able to tap the Foreign Mission Board's computer, for example, in order to receive up-to-the-minute data. As you prepare a missions sermon or a presentation for the Woman's Missionary Union meeting, you could get accurate statistics on how many missionaries serve in Ghana, what new countries have been entered in the last six months, or a report of the latest conditions in Lebanon. Or, before long, you'll call the Home Mission Board's mainframe, log on with your personal computer, and download a list of the most urgent prayer requests. Armed with that data, you'll be more precise and up-to-date when you lead the congregational prayer on Home Mission Sunday.

But, you say, wouldn't a phone call to a staff member at one of these agencies be just as good as a computer linkup? Obviously, the phone call would work all right, but with the computer you wouldn't have to take down the detailed information by hand, or record your conversation on tape for transcription later. Your data would be both accurate and immediately available. Besides, you can log on to the computer anytime, twenty-four hours a day, without concern for business hours, time zone differences, or annoying delays trying to find the appropriate personnel to give you the data. Similar scenarios with other denominational agencies, or better, an interconnected agency network, could significantly reduce research time and the volume of printed materials you might otherwise feel impelled to have on hand for such quests.

Already, Southern Baptists have at their disposal a growing data bank of helpful information gathered and maintained by the Center for Urban Church Studies in Nashville, Tennessee. Jointly sponsored by several of our Convention agencies, the Center collects data on evangelistic strategies, church growth projects, missiological studies, and demographic statistics. Along with many other items, this data is being stored in the memory of a computer and is available now, under certain restrictions, for transfer to remote computer terminals. One other source of helpful data comes from the annual church "letters" Southern Baptist congregations submit to their associations each fall. These statistics from some 30,000 churches are collected by the Convention in Nashville, and computerized by the Research Services Department, making available an immense bank of information about Southern Baptist churches. Soon, such data will be accessible through a telecommunications network by personal computer users in remote locations.

Southwestern Seminary already has its theological library catalog on line and accessible by personal computer, and will soon have a theological and biblical data base (called STABIS, Southwestern Theological and Biblical Information Service) in operation which will allow you to link up your terminal to receive information.

Teleconferencing

Another example of networking is "Teleconferencing"—bringing people together for meetings by means of connected computers. Avoiding expensive travel and wasted time, teleconferencing is growing in popularity within the business community. Like a conference phone call, everyone involved turns on his personal computer at a predetermined time, links up with a network facility, and watches his screen as the chairman calls the meeting to order and invites input. Each participant gets in their "two-cent's worth" by typing comments on his or her own keyboard, while the others simultaneously read them on their screens. The entire content of the meeting is stored in each computer's memory, so each member of the group has an identical record without the need of written minutes.

Granted, such an electronic meeting lacks the ambience and fellowship which are appealing advantages in "getting together." But you'll have to admit there are some meetings that don't have much ambience even if you're there in person. That kind of meeting would certainly be improved by the brevity and convenience of teleconferencing.

The feasibility of another facet of network communications is currently being demonstrated by programs such as CompuServe's popular CB Stimulator. In the evenings, when the rates are cheaper, thousands of subscribers log on to CompuServe Information Service, and from its menu, enter the CB program. (CB stands for citizens band, the car radio phenomenon that induced so many everyday drivers to join the truckers in "jawing" with one another on the road. Now you can do it on your computer, too.)

It works just like the CB in your car. Once you've logged on, you give yourself a "handle," indicate on the screen that you'd like to talk, and from somewhere across the anonymous world of subscribers you'll be answered by "Bluebird," or "Rubber Duck," or someone with another assumed name. Back and forth the conversation goes as long as you want to continue. Or if you prefer, you can participate in other conversations, some of which attract large numbers of participants. Go ahead, and enter in if you'd like—most computer people are friendly, and won't be annoyed by your interruption.

Surprisingly, this form of electronic gabbing is catching on like an epidemic. Thousands each night sit before the consoles of their personal computers, anonymously engaging distant persons in casual conversation. And it's all carried on in complete silence. Only the clicking cadence of the keyboard and the eerie flicker of the electronic screen give any indication of what's happening in the room where the communicator sits.

Who knows what looms ahead for a society awash in such electronic capabilities? Like any other scientific breakthrough, the results will likely be mixed: good and bad. From a minister's viewpoint there is at least some potential for good. For instance, why couldn't you organize the computer enthusiasts in your church to join the growing masses who talk to each other each night over the network, and watch for opportunities to share their faith—to witness for Christ over the network? Why not? Already, Satan has made his move to invade this new world, because increasing numbers of these late night computer conversations are x-rated. Why not penetrate that same world with a healthy Christian witness of the gospel?

Furthermore, wouldn't there be some advantages to a denominational system similar to CompuServe's CB program? If thousands are paying subscription fees and hourly charges to chat with unknown characters across the nation, wouldn't Southern Baptists welcome a denominational network which would let them talk to each other about current issues? The popularity of "letters to the editor" in our state Baptist papers, and the growing number of radio talk shows indicate a ready market for such a plan. And, since disagreements and arguments often thrive because of misunderstandings, we should be open to any innovation that encourages broader communication and understanding. Some day this kind of networking, already widespread in the secular world, will be employed by Christians. It's already happening in a few places.

In his article "Computers and Ministry" in *The Christian Ministry* magazine, Parker Rossman describes a network called TELIDON, employed by Canadian churches to keep denominational offices in touch with individual parishes.[4] Ministers and laypersons alike can turn to their computers for a list of counseling services, or a list of religious courses available, or to ask where to find churches in a new area, or to get information about current church meetings and programs. Plans are already under way through TELIDON to link not only a local church and the denominational office, but one parish to another. When a particular social or moral issue arises that should be addressed by a cooperative church effort, the computers rally members in various churches for a campaign or a plan of action.

Electronic Mail

Another networking feature that is already available is electronic mail. CompuServe, THE SOURCE, STARTEXT, and other information services offer it to their subscribers. I've tried the CompuServe "EMAIL" service, which makes it easy to read your mail. But the procedure for answering mail is so complicated that it discourages a beginner from using it. Subscribers to THE SOURCE, on the other hand, praise its "SourceMail" program because it is so easy to send messages.

If you're a subscriber to THE SOURCE, you have an ID number and a password that authorizes you to use the service. Dial the phone number for SOURCE in your area, and when the beep tells you the computer has answered, switch on your modem, and you're connected. You'll be asked for your number and password; and if all is in order, even before giving you its menu of options, THE SOURCE tells you how many letters are in your electronic mailbox. Push the keys that take you to SourceMail, and, one by one, the letters are presented to you on the screen. You can also download them into the memory of your computer for more careful reading later.

After you've read a letter, SOURCE asks if you want to answer it now. Responding with an "N" puts the letter back in your box for later. Responding with a "Y" gives you a blank screen to answer the letter immediately. Type "s" at the end of your reply and THE SOURCE sends it to the appropriate mailbox. You don't even have to insert the ID number of the person you're answering, because the computer remembers that from its letter to you. After answering the letter, delete it and go to the next one.

No need for dictating, proofreading the typed copy, signing, sealing, stamping, or taking it to the post office. Each of these steps is a discouraging obstacle in the path of someone who is a correspondence procrastinator. But with electronic mail, you can receive and send messages with lightning speed and with much less trouble. As more and more people get personal computers and subscribe to networks, electronic mail promises to become a viable alternative to Uncle Sam's struggling mail service.

Imagine what the apostle Paul could have done with electronic mail if the computer had been invented 2,000 years ago. First-century churches equipped with "ROMULUS, JR. PCs" could have logged on to the "APPIAN INFORMATION SERVICE" and could have circulated one of Paul's Pastoral Epistles instantly. All the churches of Asia could have read the letter simultaneously. If he had used a word processor, I wonder what the "autograph" of 2 Timothy would have looked like, or what effect an electric power surge in the middle of Paul's Letter to the Romans would have had.

Of course, the Holy Spirit could have transmitted God's perfect revelation by means of electronic digits on a floppy disk as well as lampblack letters on a vellum scroll. But the New Testament phrase, "In the fullness of time," suggests that in His infinite wisdom, God knew it was better to do it back then, in the simpler communications environment of the first century. Even so, I suppose Paul did face occasional interruptions such as running out of ink when the market was closed, or breaking his last quill pen. But the word processor, while presenting him with some unique challenges he never had to face, would have given him some great advantages. For that reason, I believe, had it been available then, the apostle would have enthusiastically engaged the computer in his work. That conclusion is based on the fact that under the leadership of the Spirit, Paul did employ the latest writing, duplication, and mail techniques of his day. That seems to me to validate our own use of the latest technology in ours.

The possibilities of electronic networking and the integration of computers with other telecommunications marvels brings into view incredible new horizons which we dare not overlook nor surrender to the secularists. Soon, visionary scientists will bring together all our electronic technology into a comprehensive system, connecting TV, radio, video recorder, discs, tapes, clock, cable, thermostats, and much more. Have you seen the ARETE electronic encyclopedia which already uses this kind of integration? When you look up its reference to Beethoven, for example, it not only instantly gives you the full printed text about the composer, but also plays one of his symphonies, and shows a full-color video about his birthplace and early life! One integrated videodisc has been developed that can produce 55,000 pages of interactive text in a similar fashion.[5]

Whether you use it immediately for networking or not, you should learn enough about the personal computer to be ready to take advantage of networking when, if predictions are correct, it suddenly explodes on the scene.

Notes

1. John Naisbitt, *Megatrends* (New York: Warner Books, Inc., 1984), pp. 211-229.
2. Gil Gordon quoted in "Telecommuting," *Online Today,* Vol. 3, # 3, March 1984, p. 17.
3. See "Telecommuting," *PC Weekly,* March 20, 1984, p. 37.
4. Parker Rossman, "Computers and Ministry," *The Christian Ministry,* Vol. 15, #2, March 1984, p. 11.
5. Ibid.

9
The Personal Computer and the Minister's Family

When it comes to integrating personal computers into our family life, we're really a "guinea pig" generation. Just a few years ago if someone had told you that today you would own a computer with all the power of a giant, room-size mainframe which was the norm in those days, you would have laughed with disbelief or maybe fear. But your children, growing up with computers, won't have that problem. Their generation will be used to this new technology and will use computers as comfortably and naturally as we use the telephone or the automobile. But our generation is still feeling its way. We're the guinea pigs who have to deal with the explosive entrance of computers into our homes and have to figure out for ourselves how to integrate them into family life.

You've seen those magazine ads picturing a typical, well-scrubbed American family seated in the glow of a computer screen, rapturously gazing on the new machine as though it were a newborn baby just home from the hospital. As is often the case with advertising, there is a measurable difference between that idyllic scene in the ad and the reality of your own family when you bring your computer home. Contrary to the ad, a computer is not easily shared. It's a device normally used by one person at a time for a specific task. When you buy a computer for use in your ministry and then try to involve the rest of your family in computing, it can be a no-win situation. If you do involve them, then you may create a situation where members of the family are competing for time on the machine, and you may find yourself in the market for a second computer. On the other hand, if no one is interested but you, then the rest of the family may resent the time you spend on your "new toy." It isn't as easy as the ad implies. You have to do more than just unpack the machine and gather the family around to watch it.

But in spite of the pitfalls, the potential for the computer to pull families together and improve the quality of family life is there. A New York University study has found that families with personal computers spend more time together, watch less television, and their children do more homework. The professor who guided the study of families in New York, Connecticut, and New Jersey said:

> Families appreciate each other a bit more than when dad was watching TV and the son was playing his guitar. They're spending more time together at home because they're having fun working on their computer. As more and more homes get computers, the technological revolution could alter the structure of the family.[1]

Encouraged by optimistic predictions like that, some families are making the mistake of buying computers just because it's the thing to do. In many of these cases, the computer sits unused, gathering the same dust that covers their unused Bibles. No one knows what it will do, much less how to use it. It's almost necessary for one member of the family to become "obsessed" with the computer, or at least very enthusiastic about it, to involve the rest of the family. You will probably have to be that person for your family.

If you agree that the computer can be a valuable new tool in your ministry and want the other members of your family to have computer advantages, you'll have to invest the time to learn and lead the way. You'll have to be the one who gets "hooked" on computing and who helps the family get past the initial frustration of a new electronic appliance. If you can transmit your enthusiasm to the rest of the family, you're well on the way to integrating the computer into the household and removing any reluctance or resentment they might feel.

Thomas F. McDonald, a clinical psychologist who studies how computers affect relationships, thinks it's worth the effort. He believes that learning and recreational activities have been redefined and expanded for those families whose members have embraced the home machine. Instead of passively watching television or quietly reading books—activities that can segregate families into individual mental cocoons—many computing families interact with one another and the machine. What are the primary uses a family is likely to make of a personal computer?

Games

When it comes to getting children involved, games are a good place to start. Computer games attract them on their level, teach them to type, and to interact with the computer, and, therefore, make it easier to go on to the next level. Most families with televisions have already discovered electronic games. Television game machines have become relatively inexpensive, and your children have probably already become champions at several video games. You may have tried a game or two yourself (out of a mature parental desire to interact with your children, of course), and discovered, to your surprise, that these games require a high level of dexterity, coordination, and intelligence.

Well, the personal computer plays games in much the same way a television does. You simply buy the software at the computer store, load it into your machine, and play the game, using various strokes on the keyboard. Or, if you're a real enthusiast, you can upgrade your machine. Most personal computers have an outlet into which you can plug a "joystick" controller or a "roller ball" or even a steering wheel device for auto racing games.

A color computer with a high resolution screen and sound capabilities is best for games, but even the less expensive, plain vanilla models will accept game programs on disks or tape. My Model 4P can play paddle games; popular space games; and games that let you explore an Egyptian tomb for hidden treasure, escape from an asylum, solve the mysteries of a ghostly haunted mansion, find treasure in a magic temple, or fly an airplane. There are also computer versions of games like chess, backgammon, Scrabble, and Monopoly.

In a category slightly above games, but still entertaining, are programs that let you draw or create designs on the computer screen. You can program your machine to print huge banners on rolls of computer paper with letters as tall as your printer will allow (14″ on mine). And for the musically gifted, you can compose and play songs on the computer. For input, some of these programs use a "scratch pad" device in the place of the keyboard, and thereby allow children who are too young to use the keys to play with the computer. While games help introduce your children to computers and may continue to be an important family use of your micro, you'll want to move the family to the next level as soon as possible.

Education

For most families the next level will be educational programs. Educational software of every imaginable sort is available for every age. You can buy programs that feature Donald Duck teaching children how to tell time, or Mickey Mouse helping youngsters learn sentence structure and basic writing skills, or Goofy exploring our government. Sesame Street characters will introduce numbers, history, and letters to your boys and girls. There are reading packages with illustrated readers, cassette tapes, and computer programs with spelling and vocabulary exercises for classics such as *Twenty Thousand Leagues Under the Sea* or *Moby Dick.*

Secondary math and science courses are available to enhance your student's work in physics, chemistry, quadratic equations, matrices, plane analytic geometry, or integral calculus.

Some families subscribe to the Plato Homelink Network from Control Data in order to receive educational courses and games over the telephone lines. For a modest subscription fee and hourly charge for line time, your children not only have access to Plato's 270 different programs, but they learn about computer networking by going through the process of logging on. One thing's for sure: They're not likely to get bored with so many different options to choose from.

I was really impressed with a unique educational program for older children offered by Radio Shack called Corplan. Employing realistic computerized simulations, the program helps students learn about the world of business by leading them through typical experiences they would have if they owned a company. In control of an imaginary corporation, the young entrepreneurs make quarterly decisions under varying conditions in order to maximize profits. They develop strategies in production, advertising, sales, and finance under changing conditions of taxes, labor, financial forecasts, prices, and market factors.

The program maintains complete accounting records and balance sheets for each quarter and allows the participants to raise funds by issuing bonds or additional stock shares. It even allows for emergency bank loans. (That's as realistic as most would want to get.) Think what an advantage young people going into business have if they've grown up with several years of this kind of computer simulation.

More advanced students (including Dad and Mom) can even register in the world's first electronic university, Telelearning Systems of San Francisco, California. Students purchase the "Telelearning Knowledge Module" which contains a 300 baud modem, all connections, software, and listing of course offerings. The university is accessed via telephone lines, and student and teacher can converse in real time or by electronic mail. Course topics range from business to the arts, and from parenting to gourmet cooking. In electronic "classrooms" which are open twenty-four hours a day, students attend on-line lectures, take tests, write papers, and even have private tutoring sessions with the instructor—all by means of the computer.

The use of computers in our public schools and colleges is almost universal today. Your children will be expected to be as familiar with computers by the time they graduate from high school as you were with tape recorders and typewriters. A cartoon quip I read recently illustrates this point clearly. A boy says to his father, "It's OK for you to say arithmetic is easy. You figure in your head—I have to use a computer!"

According to a survey by Talmis, a computer research firm, more than four million college students will own personal computers by 1987! Their study shows that in just one year alone, from 1982 to 1983, the number of students who owned computers tripled to nearly 750,000. It seems to me that wise parents who are aware of these impressive statistics and the inevitable trend they reveal will want their children to become computer literate by using the machines at home. If they had no other practical use than education, that would be reason enough to involve your family in the computer revolution.

Word Processing

The next use a family is most likely to make of a personal computer is word processing. Using the same software, school children can write reports and themes, Mom can write letters, and Dad can prepare his sermons. While some word processing programs are complicated and sophisticated, most are flexible and simple enough for older children to learn. Refer to chapter 2 for a description of some of the word processing software which is available today.

Home Finance Programs

Most of us identify readily with that little sign we sometimes see on a messy desk, "Tomorrow I've Got to Get Organized!" We've made that resolution a hundred times at work and probably a thousand times at home. Every time we open that drawer full of bills and receipts, we say it: "Tomorrow I've got to get organized." When we examine that stack of bank statements, most of which we have not balanced with our checkbook, we say, "Tomorrow I've got to get organized." Especially at income tax time, when we've struggled to get our return in on time, we've all said it with a slight variation: "Next year I've got to get organized."

The personal computer offers a way to neatly organize your financial transactions so you can throw away the sign on your desk and never have to make that resolution about tomorrow again. There are numerous programs marketed today to help families manage their finances, and this certainly ought to be an application to consider as you use your computer at home.

But first, lest you mistakenly assume that the computer will solve all your financial record problems, consider these factors. Home accounting programs for computers require you to enter lots of data regularly. If you're the kind of person who forgets to record checks in your checkbook or who tosses out receipts for tax-deductible expenditures, these programs probably won't be much help, unless you resolve to get better organized. Don't expect the computer to do it all without any effort on your part. On the other hand, if you're a careful record keeper, the computer can really simplify home accounting chores.

Second, home accounting programs are designed primarily to help families who have fairly complex financial needs. If you usually fill out the short form when you file your income tax returns, you probably don't need a computer to help you. A hand-held calculator will be sufficient to handle your records. Most minister's families probably fall somewhere in between the short form category and the category which requires complicated records of assets, real estate, business expenses, rental income, and multiple tax shelters. If you are in this middle class, then the computer may be just what you need to get your records under control.

Third, if your primary desire is to automatically balance your checkbook, then buying a computer is an electronic overkill. Sure, computers will balance checkbooks, but the programs I've examined would require twice as much time and effort as the old-fashioned method of doing it by hand. You not only have to write the checks and keep the stub records, but you have to enter the checks into the computer on a regular basis as well. About all the machine does is keep a running balance for you so you won't have to subtract each check manually. Believe me, it's not worth the expense and effort to buy a computer for that purpose alone.

With these considerations out in the open, let's examine what some of the popular home finance programs can do for you. First, there are many spreadsheet programs on the market today similar to the well-known VisiCalc series. In chapter 2, I described how these powerful electronic accounting programs work. Since the spreadsheet is one of the most popular business applications for a personal computer, many families use it for managing their household financial records, too. Using VisiCalc, for example, you can plan a family budget, keep records of checks, income, and expenses by an unlimited number of categories. The program automatically recalculates every column on the spreadsheet any time you make a single change in any item. So, if you use a computer spreadsheet as a church administration tool, you can bring the disk home and use it to program your family budget and other financial records, too.

However, there are an increasing number of programs designed specifically for home accounting. They track your spending, help organize your budget, account for assets and liabilities, flag tax-deductible expenses, produce income statements and balance sheets, and prepare income tax returns. One of these programs is called Dollars and Sense. (You'll have to admit, computer programmers sometimes create clever titles.) It's menu-driven, has clearly-written learner's manuals, and is simple to use. First, you're given the opportunity to create accounts by number and name, and to categorize them as an expense, income, asset, or liability. Once the accounts are in place, you then make regular entries on the screen.

Here's an example of how it works. On the first of the month, after having written the check for your house loan payment, you then enter the transaction on the screen. You can split the payment into principal and interest, and flag the interest portion as tax-deductible—that is, if the IRS will allow you the advantage of housing allowance *and* mortgage interest deductions. Be certain to stay aware of changing regulations. The program then automatically reduces your loan balance by the amount of principal you've paid, and automatically totals your interest payments for tax purposes. As your various transactions are recorded, an up-to-the-minute report of your total financial situation can be shown on the screen, or a formal financial statement can be printed for your banker.

When April 15 arrives, you won't have to sort through a year's accumulation of receipts. You'll have it all up-to-date and ready to enter in your computer's tax program, which will then calculate and print out your return on IRS forms. Most tax preparation programs provide updates each year to reflect changes in the tax code. And the expense of the tax-preparation software may be allowed as a deduction.

But I've only scratched the surface of the vast library of programs available. There are household inventory programs which organize your property by room number, item description, brand, year bought, place bought, model number, serial number, color, and cost. How long have you been putting off preparing such an inventory for insurance purposes? Well, now's your chance to get it done with the computer's help.

Do you live on a farm? Some ministers do, and there are specialized programs to help them keep track of farm machinery, soybean/corn crop yield, cow/calf herd rations, feedlot cattle management, and dozens of other farm records.

Another program helps the newspaper carrier in your family prepare and update subscriber's files and prepare billing forms. It then prints the charges on labels or envelopes to be delivered with the papers on the first of each month.

The list goes on and on. Whatever your family's financial record-keeping needs may be, the computer has a plan to help meet those needs.

Networks

With a modem attached to your home computer, its potential for helping your family is extended remarkably. For one thing, some banks are now allowing computer owners to complete their banking transactions at home. Instead of writing checks, addressing envelopes, stamping, and mailing them, bills can be paid by sitting at your terminal and typing out instructions directly to your bank.

Another example of networking involves the use of a local information service like STARTEXT in Fort Worth. It allows you to see the want ads in the daily paper the minute they're placed, well before the paper is delivered to others. Furthermore, Electronic Shopping Malls are now in operation to allow you to shop at home by means of your computer.

Using CompuServe, one of the popular national information services, your children can look up encyclopedia articles, movie reviews, and sports reports; Mom can get instant information on medical problems, economics, nutrition, and New York fashions; and Dad can receive data on the weather in any part of the world, stock reports, science articles, and the latest news from the *Washington Post.* Actually, I counted nearly 700 different subjects in CompuServe's alphabetical subject listing to which a subscriber could go in his quest for information.

Travel is one of these. Last week, for example, a couple from Detroit, Michigan, booked a seven-day Caribbean cruise that departed from Miami Beach, Florida. When they arrived, not only was a rental car waiting at the airport, they also had front-row tickets to a stage show, reservations at their favorite

Chinese restaurant, and overnight accommodations at a seaside hotel before their ship departed the next morning. That's not so unusual, except for the fact that they made all the arrangements themselves from their home through their personal computer! On-line travel services allow you to choose from thousands of vacation plans, check weather conditions and currency rates, book all your reservations, and obtain electronic confirmations twenty-four hours a day from your home.

There are even "barter services" through which vacationers can exchange their home in Texas for a villa in Rome. Subscribers can trade cottages, yachts, chalets, or recreational vehicles by posting on the computer what they have to trade and what they want in exchange. Travelers then shop for the various options and contact each other by phone, regular mail, or electronic mail.

It's obvious from this incomplete review of the limitless family uses available that the computer is not a single-purpose appliance. Because of its incredible flexibility, you should not secure one to use only as a word processor or to access CompuServe. Identify some primary purposes, yes; but then branch out into other family applications in order to capture the personal computer's full potential. That's when you begin to get your money's worth.

Notes

1. Article in *Fort Worth Star-Telegram,* May 5, 1984.
2. Thomas F. McDonald, "Living, Learning and Laboring with the Micro," *Today,* Vol. 2, No. 13, May 1983, p. 18.

10
The Minister's Computer: A Limited Tool

Since I've extolled the virtues of the personal computer with such unbridled enthusiasm, you might mistakenly assume that I'm blind to its limitations. That's not the case. Admittedly, my regard for the computer as a tool for ministry is high, but not unqualified. In fact, in the initial chapter of this book, I confessed to an inherent lack of appreciation for technology in general, and a reluctance to invite the personal computer into my life in particular. While I've overcome those aversions to become something of a computer enthusiast, I don't believe I've lost touch with reality. I know these new machines are not perfect. They have their limitations, and users must assess them from a balanced perspective.

Only a hermit could be unaware of the current computer mania. The volume of advertising for personal computers is immense. Sometimes it appears that the whole world has fallen in line behind the computer like unquestioning children following a Pied Piper. The headlong rush into computers is so universal that it's difficult to find any profession that hasn't joined the revolution.

National analysts predict that information technology will reshape society more radically than any other development in history. On this, all the experts agree. But from that point they are divided between the optimists who see the computer as a great blessing and those who see it as a great detriment. It's either an Aladdin's lamp or a Pandora's box. So while some of us rave exuberantly about the computer's potential for good, there are others who with equal exuberance rant about its potential for evil.

In fact, there's actually an anticomputer backlash developing among those who, for one reason or another, don't go along with all the hoopla about computers. Some of them object because they're afraid, and computer phobia is not easy to overcome. Increasing numbers are afraid of unemployment —fearful of being replaced by seventeen-year-old kids who've grown up with computers. What middle-aged executive isn't intimidated when he realizes that most fifth graders know more about computers than he does?

That's why a foreign language teacher I heard about no longer brings in young native children to speak to her class. When a person who's been struggling for five years to speak Japanese suddenly realizes that he will never speak it as well as that five-year-old child, a pall of gloom descends over the learning process. The same pall of gloom clouds the enthusiasm of those who see their careers threatened by a youthful generation of computer hackers.

Others fear what Bernard Ramm calls "a stratification of society." What if the new computer popularity creates a superclass of people who know digital science and who use their knowledge to control the rest of us who are electronic neophytes or, worse, ignoramuses.[1]

One victim of computer fear, a fifty-one-year-old vice-president of a medium-sized company, may be typical of many others. His department was being computerized and he couldn't cope. He bought, but could not read, computer books. He swore they were all written in some strange, non-English language he couldn't translate. He hung around computer stores, but couldn't muster up the courage to confess his fear. Finally he made an appointment with the company's psychological counselor and lamented the fact that he was too young to retire and too old to start over. "Maybe I could just die early!" he sighed.[2]

Computer phobia creates, on the one hand, some antitech

naysayers who stand about like whittlers around a potbellied stove shaking their heads at the revolution and refusing to have anything to do with it. They'll eventually join it, but not now, and never willingly. Stubbornly digging in their heels, they'll be dragged in kicking and screaming as reluctant latecomers, finally admitting there's something to this computer thing after all.

On the other hand, there are those who express their objections with a proud individualism that boasts of their refusal to be stampeded. They resolutely cling to the old ways just to be different. For example, there's a Florida bank president who resolutely refuses to read anything printed on paper with little holes along the sides!

So, while they may express their resistance in different ways, these "backlashers" are a growing force who have themselves become a new market for enterprising capitalists. One such opportunist is offering computer haters a unique product with which they can vent their disenchantment. It looks just like a desktop computer. It has a keyboard, a black screen, a swiveling base, and a long electric cord with a plug on the end. It's called the "Do-Little 1." It has no memory, no disk drives, no software, no manuals, and it costs only $29.95.

When you turn it on, bright green letters flash on the screen just like a real machine, but if you get close enough, you can see that the letters say, "I AM NOT A COMPUTER. REPEAT. I AM NOT A COMPUTER. REPEAT. I AM NOT A COMPUTER. I JUST LOOK LIKE ONE." The Do-Little 1 is being snapped up like hot cakes by people who loathe computers and who want to say by putting one on their desk, "I realize that someday I'll have to enter the computer age, but not now!"

Walter Reich expressed his frustration on the pages of *The Wilson Quarterly.*[3] He suggested (humorously, I think) that the exploding popularity of personal computers in the United States is actually the result of a Soviet conspiracy. In 1951 it seems the U.S. had a secret project called "Bar Harbor" whereby they flew 800 C-54s over the Russian cities of Rostov and Vladivostok and dumped 200,000 pairs of nylon hose, four million packs of cigarettes, 35,000 Toni wave kits, 20,000 yo-yos, and 10,000 wristwatches. The thought was that deluging the deprived masses with these consumer marvels would cause them to forsake the drab, Spartan philosophy of Communism for the bright promises of private enterprise.

It didn't work, but according to Reich, the Soviets have retaliated for our underhanded attempt with a "Bar Harbor" project of their own. It was the Soviets who secretly financed those young electronic experts who, out of their backyard laboratories, began flooding our country with personal computers. And, sure enough, just as the Soviets suspected, the energies and talents of our brightest executives began to be sapped by their hypnotic involvement with the new electronic toys. Because of the Soviet conspiracy, our executives are now spending twenty hours a week doing precisely and elegantly with their computers what they used to do adequately and plainly in five. The devious enemy plan is working, says Reich, because businessmen, who until recently worked happily with paper and pencil, are now falling all over each other at the local computer store to buy up the latest equipment so they can spend thirty-five hours a week in wasted digital bliss.

He suggests, as a countermeasure, that we might endow numerous law schools in Russia to teach a whole generation of Soviets the art of incessant litigation. Or we could have the *Voice of America* bombard their innocent citizens with regular broadcasts of Monday night football!

Tongue in cheek, yes. But there is enough truth in the concerns of the anticomputer backlash that we should listen and temper our enthusiasm with some healthy skepticism. Especially since it's so easy for people who are unfamiliar with computers to be awed by these miraculous new inventions. There's a certain aura about a computer printout that entices people to believe anything it says. They assume that if it came from a computer it must be the final, authoritative word.

We unintentionally propagate that myth of infallibility when we use terms like, "the computer did" or "the computer said." Recognizing this natural tendency to "deify" the computer, we who know better should be the first to admit that it's no more than an imperfect machine with obvious limitations. We should also admit that some of the concerns raised by those who are unimpressed by electronics are legitimate.

One appropriate concern, especially for ministers, is the potential in computers for depersonalization. Nobody wants to be dehumanized. No one wants to be reduced to an anonymous digit on somebody's computerized data base. The select few who received invitations to attend the gala opening of the Museum of Modern Art in New York this year must have felt privileged until they learned how they were chosen.

The "status committee" that selected the 9,180 who received invitations, thereby judging them as deserving and consigning the rest of us 230 million to the social outback, was not only snobbish, but inhuman, too. Those invited were chosen by an IBM System 38 computer! When we hear that, we almost feel a sense of pride in *not* being chosen!

Naisbitt alerted us to the dangers of depersonalization in the information age when he named one of his megatrends: "High tech/High touch." As the new technology emerges, there arises a counterbalancing human drive for personal relationships, personal worth, and personal identity. In an informal conference recently, I heard the noted author of *Megatrends* enlarge on this thesis. He described the stubborn resistance to depersonalization that has arisen since he wrote his book. A few years ago, Naisbitt remembered, most of us were always impressed when we received a "typed" letter, particularly if it was typed on an IBM executive typewriter. The letter somehow looked impressive and important. Now, he says, handwritten mail has the highest impact! We have become so jaded by the impersonalized professionalism of typed letters, that the personal, handwritten note is now the exciting thing.

He's right. Mechanization has a way of robbing us of precious personal values. When that happens, the price of technology is too high. For example, the computer has given us the convenience of nationwide telephone floral services which we can call twenty-four hours a day, seven days a week. But is it worth it? What does it really mean to be able to ask that a flower arrangement we can't see be delivered by a total stranger to a door several hundred miles away? What does it mean to the telephone "florist" who might arrange for the transfer of several hundred bouquets per day, but never sees a single flower? Perhaps the cost of that computerized bouquet is more than we've calculated.

Rene Guenon said, "Servant of the machine, the man must become a machine himself, and thenceforth his work has nothing really human in it."[4] And Sydney J. Harris warned, "The real danger is not that computers will begin to think like men, but that men will begin to think like computers."[5]

But if an uncritical worship of computers is evil, an uncritical rejection of computers is worse. Wouldn't it be tragic if our corrective for computer abuse ended up being worse than the abuse—a cure worse than the disease? Do you remember the nineteenth-century Luddites who feared the encroaching industrial revolution? Mobs of these British workers went about smashing the machines which were the new inventions of their day. There may be some frustrated iconoclasts today who would gladly rally behind twentieth-century Luddites bent on destroying all these pesky new computers, but that won't work. The information age is on us, and the computers which that information age has spawned are here to stay, like them or not. Neither worship nor rejection is the proper response. Balance—that's what we need.

So let me conclude by calling on contemporary Christian ministers to take a balanced, common-sense approach in their use of the personal computer. It is indeed a valuable new tool for ministers. But it is *only* a tool. It can't take the place of a minister, nor should it be allowed to replace the human, personal qualities of the ministry. It is said that one machine can do the work of fifty ordinary persons, but no machine can do the work of one minister. It can enhance the quality of his work, enlarge the capacity of his work, and improve the organization of his work. But if the minister engages the computer as an end in itself, or if he becomes so mechanized that he loses the personal touch, or the value of individual worth, then the machine quickly becomes his enemy. The need is for balance.

In a humorous article in *The Christian Century,* Methodist minister William H. Willimon expressed this plea for balance convincingly.[6] He tells how he decided to be the pastor of the first computerized church. You've heard of the electronic church. Well, pastor Willimon organized the Microchip Church. A full line of computer equipment was installed, and the entire membership was added to a data base along with the minutest details of their lives. And now, every day the computer pulls people's names and makes a personal call to them (using a recording of the pastor's voice) which goes like this:

> Hello, (name inserted). This is your pastor. Just wanted you to know that I was thinking about you in my prayer time this morning. Isn't this the day you married (or divorced, were robbed, graduated, got certified, were promoted, or fired, or 200 other categories of human experience) last year? Why, certainly I remembered. How could I forget? Good-bye (X).

Willimon's imaginary microchip church has an on-line connection with the local police station, family court, credit bureau, and utility companies. They receive a printout each day of everyone who moves into town, everyone who is arrested, all divorce filings and child custody decisions, and upcoming cases in civil court. Talk about matching evangelism with human needs! Why imagine the impression this church makes on a family who has just had the lights turned off for nonpayment of their electric bill when a church team shows up hours later offering to have prayer with them.

The church computer can also influence legislative action by sending to a politician hundreds of letters signed by members of the congregation protesting some pending legislation. But that's not nearly as exciting as the action the pastor took when the bishop tried to move him last year because of the complaints of a group of malcontents in his church. With one touch of a key, guess who got a thousand personal letters expressing shock and dismay? Some people sit around and wait for the Holy Spirit to work in guiding their vocations, but the microchip pastor prefers to peck out a few programs that make things happen when they ought to. For example, with the computer, he can send personalized sympathy cards and get-well cards to any district superintendent in the conference!

Listen to the testimony of this computerized pastor.

> While other pastors are pounding the pavement, knocking on doors, and beating out sermons, I have just sent letters to every charismatic female over the age of 35 with a college degree who owns her own home and has an income of over $30,000 a year, to tell each one personally about our special upcoming Labor Day service. Think of what Martin Luther could have done with this technology!

Thanks, William Willimon, for what I believe is the most eloquent plea I've heard for balance in the minister's use of technology. Because they know man's basic need is spiritual; because they know man is saved only by faith in Christ, not by machines; because of their sensitive awareness of the value of personhood; and because they've been called to raise prophetic voices in this age of technology; ministers are the ones who are best-equipped today to teach people how to use computers wisely. They must show the computer age how to master technology rather than serve it blindly.

Billy Graham's words are a timely reminder.

> We have learned how to harness the power of the atom, but very few of us have learned how to develop fully the power of prayer. We have not yet learned that a person is more powerful on his knees than behind the most sophisticated machine we have ever developed.[7]

The personal computer: a new tool for the ministry. Yes, but it is a limited tool, to be used with balanced common sense.

Notes

1. See "The Computer Revolution," *Eternity,* February 1983, p. 21.
2. John Bear, *The Computer Wimp* (Berkeley, Calif.: Ten Speed Press, 1982), p. 239.
3. Walter Reich, *The Wilson Quarterly,* Spring 1984, p. 167.
4. Quoted in "The Machine as Technique," *Epiphany,* Vol. 4, No. 1, Fall 1983, p. 13.
5. Bear, p. 244.
6. William Willimon, "The Microchip Church," *The Christian Century,* January-June 1983, p. 608.
7. Quoted in J. H. Foegen, "The Human Implications of Computers," *The Christian Century,* February 22, 1984, p. 199.

Conclusion

If my purpose in writing this book has been fulfilled, you are at least interested in the possibility of using the personal computer in your work as a minister. You may even have resolved to jump in and learn about computers, if for no other reason than to keep up with the exploding revolution going on around us. In the first chapter, I gave some suggestions for self-learning and described the numerous seminars and courses on computer use being offered by secular educational institutions. These will be helpful for your understanding of using a computer. However, if you want to focus your computer education on its specific application for Christian ministry, you'll probably find the courses offered in a theological seminary to be more to the point.

Many seminaries are offering an increasing number of credit courses dealing with the minister's use of computers. I know this is the case at Southwestern Seminary. Usually these courses can be audited by students who might not be interested in pursuing another degree. However, these courses are probably scheduled over the months of a regular semester, and it might be impractical for you to enroll. Should this be the case, check to see if courses are offered through a continuing education program or in a center near you.

There are many computers on the market that will meet your needs as a minister. As examples, I have described the equipment I use and have mentioned other items currently available. Other useful computers will be announced as the technology continues to develop. I do not know what kind of equipment you might choose; I am confident that a computer will help ministers do their work more efficiently in many areas. My hope throughout this book has been that you will be open to ways that will help all of us spread the good news of Jesus Christ more effectively. I am convinced that the personal computer is a tool that can help ministers. I hope you will consider the possibility of using a computer to help you do the work of ministry God has called you to do.